GW00384234

I Remember King Kong
(The Boxer)

Denis Hirson

First published in 2004 by Jacana Media (Pty) Ltd.
5 St Peter Road
Bellevue 2198
Johannesburg
South Africa

Reprinted April 2005

© Denis Hirson, 2004

All rights reserved.

ISBN 1-77009-032-0

Cover design by Orange Juice
Cover photo by Antoine Lermuzeaux
Set in Bononi 11/auto
Printed by Pinetown Printers

See a complete list of Jacana titles at www.jacana.co.za
Share your memories at www.jacana.co.za/iremember

For all those people who share these memories, and in particular the residents of 6, 8th Avenue, Melville; Piney Thatch Farm, Honeydew; and Trematon Place, Parktown, in the late 1960s and early 1970s.

To the memory of Jenny Schoon and Rick Turner.

With thanks to Robert Berold, Stephen Clingman, Jon Cook and Julian Kramer.

"Sometimes life's greatest treasures come in the flimsiest, most fleeting of forms. Take Denis Hirson's superlative new memoir. Who would ever guess that beneath the Chappies bubblegum cover of this paperback lurks one of the most poetic and timeless odes to growing up in South Africa?"

– Alex Dodd, *Sunday Times*

"What will draw many readers to the book is its affectionate tone. White South Africans, or white children at any rate, had a baffled innocence mixed in with their violence and racism, and it is this innocence which Hirson salvages so well. *I Remember King Kong (The Boxer)* is an entertaining and poignant testimony. For those (including the next generation of white kids) who are not sure if whites living under apartheid were human, this is a wonderful book to read."

– Robert Berold, *The Sunday Independent*

"Just how did (Hirson) manage to sustain a high level of artistic engagement through a repetitive choice? Somewhere in (his) answer to this question will be the miracle of (this) achievement. Long before I got to the postscript, I participated in the miracle of literary incantation. My doubts having been swept away by the third page, I began to enjoy the recall of memory through instantaneous vignettes of my own. The 'absence' of narrative (gives) birth to numerous narratives that come at you like music."

– Njabulo S. Ndebele

Contents

I remember "French kissing" and figuring out it must have
something to do with the tongue since there isn't
anything else in the mouth except teeth.

– Joe Brainard

I remember that in Monopoly, the Avenue de Breteuil is
green, the Avenue Henri-Martin is red,
and the Avenue Mozart is orange.

– Georges Perec

There is so much Everything
    that Nothing is hidden quite nicely.

– Wislawa Szymborska

I remember the grown-up feeling of going to a cinema with plush carpeting and walls and curtains in front, and being shown to your seat by an usherette with a torch in the middle of the afternoon.

I remember coming out and wondering why it still seemed to be the middle of the afternoon.

I remember watching *Jailhouse Rock*, and thinking that Elvis Presley couldn't possibly be serious about all the hip movements and twisted faces he made when he sang.

I remember being at a party full of adult-sized ducktails with Brylcreemed quiffs, leather jackets and stove-pipe trousers. They went into the street to play a game of king stingers and threw the tennis ball as if they were trying to kill each other.

I remember the sting of a wet tennis ball.

I remember when tennis balls were fluffier, and almost white.

I remember the cinema ad for Brylcreem in which Gary Player ran his fingers through his hair.

I remember the sweet oily smell of Brylcreem in its squat glass jar.

I remember the commotion in a Yeoville bioscope during matinée performances.

I remember some cinemas in the middle of town: His Majesty's, The Empire and The Colosseum.

I remember Talent Contests.

I remember The Three Stooges, and the *Carry On* films.

I remember travelling into town on a cream and red double-decker bus, and the delay when the conductor had to reconnect the runners to the overhead lines, using a long bamboo rod that he slid out from the undercarriage.

I remember that to ring the bell for the next stop, you had to pull a leather cord that was loosely strung along the ceiling, and the panic of not being able to get the bell to ring at all.

I remember that the conductor had books of different coloured cardboard tickets and a shiny silver change distributor on a leather shoulder strap.

I remember worrying that, when I grew up, there wouldn't be boys of my generation who wanted to be bus conductors.

I remember the sign in the bus, at the foot of the stairs: DO NOT SPIT/MOENIE SPOEG NIE.

I remember boys going around saying "Moenie spoeg nie!" to each other with deep spooky voices and a gargle at the end of "spoeg".

I remember the black frieze just below the ceiling in our classroom: of the veld at night, with umbrella trees and girls carrying pots on their heads.

I remember a story our teacher read us at the end of the school day about a family that lived in a tree.

I remember walking around outside a classroom before a spelling test, trying to get the letters of the word "b-e-a-u-t-i-f-u-l" in the right order.

I remember that our teacher helped us with the spelling of the word "eye" by making it into a face on the board, with eyeballs in the "e's" and nostrils in the tail of the "y".

I remember the tune my father taught me to help string together the letters "M–i-s-s-i-s-s-i-p-p-i".

I remember our little orange Schonell spelling book.

I remember the board monitor going outside to beat a cloud of dust from the duster with a ruler.

I remember the Star Chart in our classroom.

I remember that our teacher's "pet" had to tease her hair with a comb she kept in the drawer of her desk.

I remember the girl who enticed me under a table in her bedroom and said she would show me hers if I showed her mine.

I remember that after the inspection she said she wouldn't marry me. Marriage wasn't what I had in mind, but this still came as a bit of a shock.

I remember five or six of us making hooting noises as we jumped from rock to rock in a big garden, holding jam tins filled with our own excrement, and broken aloe leaves with gluey magical juice.

I remember the ticklish feeling of a songololo in the palm of my hand, and the bitter smell it left behind.

I remember going on walks and collecting as many different kinds of leaves as possible, pressing them in a book, and later wondering what to do with them.

I remember the soapy-clean smell of our primary school library.

I remember asking our Grade Two teacher if there was a special kind of chalk for drawing dotted lines.

I remember the small red and yellow cardboard counters with black dots on them, divided in two like the face of a domino, that we used in arithmetic.

I remember the sudden, urgent need to pee in the middle of an arithmetic test.

I remember my father telling me not to "pee like a horse" into the water at the bottom of the toilet bowl.

I remember that our teacher poured plaster of Paris into a saucer, and that I drew a fish in it while it was still wet.

I remember miniature groceries; also, miniature drinks of everything from Coca-Cola to Johnny Walker whisky. You could get them from people who had been on planes.

I remember that the night the first sputnik flew over Johannesburg I went outside to try and spot it. Every star seemed to be moving.

I remember Yuri Gagarin's face framed by the visor of his helmet, and Laika the dog sitting in a space capsule.

I remember thinking that gold was discovered on the Witwatersrand by someone who had accidentally kicked over a solid, gleaming nugget of gold.

I remember that two or three people all called George discovered gold. The surname of one of them was Honiball.

I remember one of the old boundary stones of Johannesburg, on Boundary Road near the Louis Botha Avenue fire station.

I remember my great aunt Essie's blue Fiat, with black rubber running boards and headlamps sticking out on either side of the hood.

I remember sitting at the back while she was driving down Louis Botha Avenue, humming elaborate home-made tunes to her and then announcing that they were by Bach.

I remember her unfailing response: "Mhmm".

I remember the mixed smell of talcum powder, deep red lipstick, fresh hairdo and Rothman's blue cigarette smoke.

I remember stockings with seams down the back, shiny black leather bags, problems with piles, and cigarette holders with gold glitter stuck in the plastic.

I remember that we picked up a black woman who was walking down Louis Botha Avenue during a bus strike. She was wearing a blanket and eating a banana.

I remember second-class bus-stops, overloaded dirty green Putco buses, and the bus-stop song in *King Kong*.

I remember that, as far as I was concerned, the original *King Kong* was about a champion township boxer who killed the woman he loved and later committed suicide by drowning himself in a dam at Diepkloof prison. The film, about an ape who kidnapped a beautiful woman, must have stolen its name from the play.

I remember thinking that the policemen surrounding King Kong when he sang to the judge about wanting to die were not actors at all.

I remember when Lucky the gangster came on and the whole stage went red.

I remember that Miriam Makeba was "discovered" by Harry Belafonte.

I remember Lemmy Special's penny-whistle music.

I remember boys singing "Oh dear, what should I do, my baby's black and I'm feeling blue"; also "Baby won't you hold my gland" and "There she was just awalkin' down the street singin' 'Do what Daddy did to Mommy to get me'."

I remember choosing the first girl I said I was in love with when everyone had to have someone to be in love with. There was no question of actually mentioning this to *her*.

I remember how, afterwards, everything about her – her smile, her freckles, her achievements in netball and her big pink house behind its split-pole fence – made her mysterious and completely unattainable.

I remember that there was always a hole in my school jacket pocket, and that sweets came unstuck from the lining encrusted with dirt and navy blue fluff.

I remember the sinking, creamy feeling of melted chocolate in a pocket.

I remember square chewy pink sweets that you could buy at the tuck-shop, and a girl who always used to chew them till her tongue looked sharp and phosphorescent.

I remember that in winter at primary school we were served a ladleful of hot chocolate in an aluminium mug; in summer there were little glass bottles of cold milk and orange juice.

I remember standing in a group at nursery school singing "The farmer's in the dell" and waiting to be chosen.

I remember standing alone in an old cracked tennis court with honeysuckle coming in through the fence and the sun pouring down while I played with sticky, bush-tailed heads of grass.

I remember that a mouse bit a hole through my brown cardboard nursery-school case.

I remember all of us lying outside during rest period, on blue canvas stretchers under the trees.

I remember the Nelsrust Dairy delivery-man, and the tinkle of milk bottles in his bicycle carrier.

I remember twirling a silver milk-bottle top across a room.

I remember balsa-wood gliders. Some of them had propellers that wound up with an elastic band.

I remember making kites using dowel sticks and green twine, brightly coloured tissue paper, and long tails tied with ribbons of cloth from my grandmother's sewing basket.

I remember the crisp sound of wind in tissue paper, and the two awful, inevitable moments when the kite either nosedived to the ground or was fatally mauled by the branches of a tree.

I remember pear-shaped wooden spinning tops with pointed metal noses, and boys trying to peg a top by whirling a second one down against it.

I remember plastic flying saucers, and perilous expeditions onto neighbours' roofs to retrieve them.

I remember the Superman programme on the radio that began with a voice saying "Up, up, and awaaaaay!"

I remember the little square paper label stuck onto the crust of Atlas bread-loaves, with a picture of Atlas bearing the world on his back.

I remember slices of Atlas bread shining with butter, peanut butter, Marmite and syrup.

I remember never understanding why, if the world was really spinning, we didn't fall off. Then my father gave me a demonstration, a ball cupped in his hand and his arm bowling fast without the ball flying loose. After that I understood even less.

I remember that Reg Park was Mr. Universe, and that later he made Bokkie garden furniture.

I remember the pills against polio that we queued up for in our school hall. They were large, white and sickly sweet, with a very soft centre.

I remember fathers projecting films during birthdays onto glistening grainy white pull-down screens, and the moment before the film when everyone stuck their hands in the light-beam of the projector.

I remember Kirk Douglas in *The Last Sunset*, and looking around when the lights went on to see who had been crying.

I remember:
Happy birthday to you,
You belong in the zoo,
You look like a monkey
And you act like one too.

I remember "Nog 'n piep!"

I remember marquees in gardens for weddings and barmitzvahs.

I remember Progressive Party and United Party marquees outside schools during elections, and people sitting inside and outside them, eating chicken salad and having drinks.

I remember red pellets against snails and slugs, and dead snails under agapanthus leaves.

I remember D.D.T.

I remember Kirchoff's, the gardening shop, with its sharp smell of new rubber and canvas.

I remember silkworms, puries and stripies, four for a cent, and the pleasure of stabbing a shirt box with the prongs of a fork so they could breathe.

I remember swollen silkworms disappearing behind their cocoons, cocoons with wet edges where the moths had bitten their way out, moths coupling tail to tail, and the problem of knowing when exactly the eggs, in their box under the bed, were going to hatch.

I remember the terrible sound of tearing silk threads when you tried to open the box and a cocoon was being spun between the base and the lid.

I remember the smell of mulberry leaves rotting against damp cardboard.

I remember braces fitted with pink plastic palates, and the food that got stuck in them.

I remember Maynard's soft wine-gums, little wine-gums the size of a pencil rubber, tubes of hard goose-pimpled gums, and marshmallow fish that you clamped between your teeth and pulled till they stretched apart.

I remember Jeremy Taylor singing:
> Ag pleez Daddy won't you take us to the drive-in,
> All six seven of us, eight nine ten,
> We wanna see the flick about Tarzan and the ape-men,
> An' when the show is over you can bring us back again.
>
> Pop-corn, chewing-gum, peanuts an' bubble-gum,
> Ice-cream, Candy-floss and Eskimo Pie,
> Ag Daddy how we miss nigger balls and liquorice,
> Pepsi-Cola, ginger-beer and Canada Dry.

I remember wondering why everyone at school suddenly seemed to know off by heart a song that I hadn't even heard of.

I remember the Jewish Orphanage at the top of Oxford Road, and the time when the orphans had to have their heads shaved because of ringworm.

I remember that divorce ended in something horrible called a "broken home", and that children of divorced parents were somehow tainted.

I remember Hayley Mills in *The Parent Trap*, and wondering how they managed to film her twice.

I remember that I had to have a candle burning in my room, or at least a light on in the passage, before I could fall asleep.

I remember:
    Here comes the candle to light you to bed,
    Here comes the chopper to chop off your head,
and the terrible pleasure of being caught which was at least as great as the pleasure of escaping.

I remember tonsilitis, and the liquid that was boiled in a pot on a gas ring in the middle of my room, filling the air with warm sweet fog.

I remember friends of mine being sent off to hospital to have their tonsils out. One of them told me he was allowed to eat a lot of ice-cream afterwards to soothe the pain.

I remember that our maid's bed was raised on bricks to keep the tokoloshe away.

I remember the question of what to do about bed bugs in the maid's room, and the pumps of poison that looked like rockets and let out a delayed hiss.

I remember pictures of St. Bernards with little barrels of rum strapped to their necks, walking up to people who were lying half- buried in the snow.

I remember that for a few weeks I tried praying before I went to sleep.

I remember:
> How many miles to Babylon?
> Four score miles and ten.
> Can I get there by candle-light?
> Yes, and back again.

I remember a glossy-haired young teacher fervently trying to teach the whole primary school how to really sing *The Lord's Prayer*, standing on the stage, making arm movements like a traffic-cop to show us which direction our lips should be going.

I remember a teacher trying to convince me that it was possible to suppress a sneeze, because "that's what sailors used to do during inspection in the Royal Navy."

I remember a group of boys threatening to polish the balls of one of their friends with black shoe polish if he was selected to be head-boy.

I remember the shields of the four Houses hanging above the stage in our primary-school hall: red with a golden crown for Alfred, yellow with a plume for Bede, blue with an open book for Caedmon, and green with a tall church hat for Dunstan.

I remember prefect badges, and a head-girl called Claudia whose hair was so blonde it had a halo.

I remember boys who had left primary school the year before swaggering back in their new high-school uniforms.

I remember water pistols, pistols that shot little silver balls, and cap-guns with pink rolls of caps.

I remember exploding those caps by hitting them with a hammer.

I remember blood blisters.

I remember grass burns, green grass stains on knee-caps, and blue bruises that turned yellow.

I remember itchy bites that had to be scratched till the blood ran, and mosquito battlefields on the wall.

I remember that at my first primary school the headmaster arranged boxing matches for boys who had been fighting with each other.

I remember mothers screaming and stamping at the ring-side while their sons were in the middle of a boxing tournament.

I remember the face of Dr. Verwoerd streaming with blood on the front page of the newspaper after David Pratt shot him at the Rand Easter Show.

I remember seeing my Standard Two teacher sunbathing in a bikini at Hartbeespoort Dam that same week-end. She looked up and said: "What are *you* doing here?"

I remember one child in a class of eight- or nine-year-olds distractedly waving a boa during our school concert, while they all sang:
    She had an itsy bitsy teeny weeny
    Yellow polka dot bikini,
    That she wore for the first time today.

I remember the shivering thrill of being in a class-room at night with the rest of the class, playing games no one could concentrate on while waiting to go across to the hall for the school concert.

I remember the Tower Of Light at the Rand Easter Show where lost children could go, and the searchlight beams swinging across Johannesburg at night.

I remember that feeling when you visited a foreign pavilion at the Rand Easter Show, like walking into a polished new country.

I remember Portuguese greengrocers, Greek cafés, and the Lebs of Highlands North who were supposed to be armed to the teeth.

I remember the hostel for Greek and Portuguese boys next to our high-school.

I remember L.M., L.M. Radio, and L.M. prawns.

I remember a Portuguese restaurant in Manzini where you could sit in a private nook, eat prawns and drink Portuguese white wine.

I remember the dancing and the bazooki music in *Zorba the Greek*, and Anthony Quinn saying to Alan Bates: "God has a very big heart, but there is one sin he will not forgive: when a woman calls a man to her bed and he will not go."

I remember how Irene Papas was stoned. And Johannesburg's indignant Greek community trying to have the film banned.

I remember Tsafendas.

I remember imagining that Tsafendas arrived during a parliamentary session wearing white gloves, ceremoniously held out a shining silver dagger on a velvet cushion, and then stabbed Verwoerd with it.

I remember hearing that Tsafendas said a tapeworm in his stomach told him to do it.

I remember front-page newspaper photos of members of the Portuguese-speaking fishing community of Tristan da Cunha, arriving in South Africa by the boatload after a volcanic eruption had shaken their island.

I remember when fishnet clothing was in fashion, especially fishnet bikinis.

I remember examining a photo in the paper of a woman at the beach wearing a "topless" with shoulder straps coming down over the nipples, and feeling cheated.

I remember Hillary on the radio singing:
    Picking up pebbles
    And throwing them into the sea,
and also
    It is the evening of the da-a-a-ay,
    I sit and watch the children pla-a-a-ay.

I remember boys wearing buffed bronze bullets and little multi-coloured plexiglass surfboards around their necks, and black nylon strands of shark-net around their wrists.

I remember charms, scoobidoos, jacks and cat's cradle.

I remember hula hoops, around the waist, up around the arms, down to the thighs and back again.

I remember Irish lines, and handwriting competitions that a girl called Merle Korp always won.

I remember how you had to put a finger between two words when you were writing to get the spacing right.

I remember inkwells and bits of blotting paper stuck in them; brightly painted, varnished wooden dipping pens with cork at the nib end, bent nibs and the disaster of spattered ink.

I remember that inky fingers smelt a bit like blood.

I remember noticing a short boy who walked with his shoes turned far outward like flippers and another boy who walked with his shoes turned so far inward it was a miracle he didn't trip himself up. After that I practised trying to walk with my shoes pointed straight ahead.

I remember horror stories about what happened to people with ingrown toenails.

I remember leaving the marble patch in a hurry at the end of big break, stamping dust out of my sandals and beating it out of the seat of my trousers, and the sound of marbles when you run with them.

I remember cat's eyes, glassies, puries, smokies, ironies, ghoens; ghoen-ghoen tish, drops, two's, castles, tens, twenties; shoe-boxes with numbers written above square mouse-holes telling you how many marbles you could win if yours went through.

I remember marbles in bank bags, lunch boxes, biscuit tins, plastic-lined swimming bags; marbles bulging in the lining of a pocket that was sticking out of a pair of shorts.

I remember the way girls bunched their skirts into their panties when they did handstands and cartwheels.

I remember:
>What's the time?
>Half past nine,
>Hang your broekies
>On the line.

I remember that the first time I kissed a girl on the lips, she was asleep. Later, I kept a secret look-out on her to see if she knew.

I remember wearing a protective box when I played cricket for the first time, and feeling a bit funny about the bulge when I went out to bat.

I remember Graeme Pollock, Peter Pollock, Eddie Barlow, Mike Procter and Colin Bland from Rhodesia, "the best fielder in the world".

I remember Charles Fortune's cricket commentaries on the wireless, his empire accent and elaborate time-filling descriptions of the weather and the crowd.

I remember the weather report for shipping after the news, and the sudden sternness when the announcer proclaimed: "There is a gale warning. I repeat: there is a gale warning."

I remember the dead voice that read the *Current Affairs* report.

I remember the high-pitched tweeting sound of the wireless when you changed frequencies.

I remember the smell of a hot wireless, and dusty light-bulbs burning behind the cloth-covered front.

I remember the "View-Master" and its cardboard disks of tiny 3-D slides.

I remember *The Living Desert*, especially the tarantula, the rattlesnake and the bobcat at the top of the cactus.

I remember wanting to catch a Goliath beetle, the biggest beetle in Africa.

I remember *Little Black Sambo*.

I remember golliwogs.

I remember when you couldn't say:
    Eeny meeny miny mo,
    Catch a nigger by his toe,
    If he hollers let him go,
    Eeny meeny miny mo
any more.

I remember that *Black Beauty* was banned until the censors realized they had made a mistake.

I remember when someone's garden was dug up by the police in a search for banned books.

I remember a mournful Afrikaans poem about a black girl, a pool and a crocodile.

I remember that when black women took off their doeks or bonnets their hair looked naked.

I remember the girls' high-school where peanuts were banned from the tuck-shop because they were supposed to be sexually stimulating.

I remember dirty pictures being handed around at high-school.

I remember wondering what exactly the "intercourse" part of sexual intercourse meant.

I remember thinking that sex would be so much more clean and pure if there wasn't all that pubic hair.

I remember the procession of men who jumped off the coal truck and through our back gate bearing shiny black bags of coal and orange sacks of sliced pine logs.

I remember the dustbin men running after the dustbin truck which was always just beyond their reach.

I remember black men entering back gates to visit the maid, unacknowledged by anyone in the garden apart from the dog.

I remember my father raging at our neighbours' young son for calling a black man "boy".

I remember white male drivers asking the petrol pump attendant to "Fill her up sharp-sharp, O.K. chief?"

I remember dusty diamond-mesh burglar proofing, and bells you could press in all the bedrooms.

I remember the broken window panes of maids' rooms stuffed with yellowing newspaper.

I remember whites in the kitchen asking their maids what the weather was going to be like that day.

I remember dirty jokes about Mary and her little lamb, and Mary and her little duck.

I remember elephant jokes, including one about an elephant upside down in a bowl of custard.

I remember "Knock knock" jokes.

I remember climbing up the brick stairs to get onto the elephant's back for a ride at the zoo.

I remember the "elephant conductor's" sharp iron prod, and the way the stretch of grass and trees beyond the cages seemed to turn wild as the elephant went shambling along.

I remember the yellow plastic arrow that shot out from the side of cars to indicate that you were turning right. Also, the arm motion as if you were stirring air below the driver's window to indicate that you were turning left.

I remember traffic patrols of primary school pupils with serious faces wearing sashes and bearing a stop sign on a pole.

I remember that when the middle-aged lady who was my driving teacher produced some plastic toy cars to show me how to park, it made me think of stories about couples therapists using plastic dolls to enlighten their patients.

I remember that you always had to check the oil and water.

I remember when it was quite common to see someone changing a tyre at the side of the road.

I remember cars stopping along the road and people getting out to have a good look at accidents, especially over the weekend.

I remember the way men would urgently encourage a woman driver to manoeuvre through a narrow space by saying: "Come on lady, you could get the Queen Mary through there!"

I remember a rush-hour driver near the zoo drawing a gun and going up to the car in front of him because he thought it was advancing too slowly.

I remember the giant clock in a flower-bed at Joubert Park, with ugly dark-leafed plants growing in the minute and hour hands.

I remember the problem of over-winding your watch, or forgetting to wind it; the problem of steamed up watch-faces, and trying to get a watch to show the right date.

I remember expandable metal watch-straps that caught the hair of the wrist.

I remember watch-makers with monocles sitting hard at work behind their shop-windows.

I remember Indian tailors.

I remember shops that sold balls of wool and knitting needles.

I remember when knitting machines came to Johannesburg.

I remember that one of the Lion Lager lions opposite the Jan Smuts Avenue entrance to Wits flicked its orange neon tail at night.

I remember that a "brown cow" is a mixture of milk and Coca-Cola.

I remember a black and white photograph in an old encyclopaedia showing all the things found in an ostrich's stomach, including a pocket watch and chain, spread out on a creased tarpaulin.

I remember Ripley's *Believe It Or Not.*

I remember stamps from places I had never heard of, like Andorra, Aden, Trinidad and Tobago, British Honduras and Rwanda-Burundi; also, stamps from somewhere called S.A.A.R. that made me think of the South African Railways.

I remember Stanley Gibbon's stamp catalogues, stamp hinges and tweezers, watermarks, and blotting paper with medical ads on the other side.

I remember that swopping stamps was fine, but buying them in cellophane packets seemed like cheating.

I remember Swop Shops.

I remember that when I heard students say they were swotting I thought of flies.

I remember the problem with air-letters: they had no detachable stamps.

I remember that if you filled in your name and address on an air-letter, "the authorities" would be able to identify you, which could cause problems. If you didn't fill in your name and address they might just get suspicious, which could also cause problems.

I remember letters that arrived in our post-box steamed open, and (badly) stuck back down with sticky tape.

I remember red-lined telegrams with the message stuck on in white strips.

I remember the white postman with his leather pouch, and the black man behind him lugging the canvas post-bag.

I remember:
    Do your balls hang low?
    Can you swing them to and fro?
    Can you tie them in a knot?
    Can you tie them in a bow?
    Can you sling them over your shoulder
    Like a continental soldier?
    Do your balls hang low?

I remember that the double lines down the side of a tennis court were called "tram-lines".

I remember when the sand courts of the Northern suburbs were dug up one by one and replaced by green all-weather courts.

I remember Cliff Drysdale, Bob Hewitt, and Frew McMillan in his floppy white hat; also, people mentioning the name of Eric Sturgess with awe.

I remember when Ken Rosewall, Roy Emerson, Pierre Barthes and perhaps Rod Laver visited Johannesburg for an exhibition match. They all looked so *clean.*

I remember when professional tennis players were impostors. The real ones were amateurs.

I remember white or khaki safari suits, and then the fashion for various pastel shades, with long socks to match.

I remember when the colour khaki was everywhere: school uniforms, socks, overalls, police, cadets, scouts, soldiers, farmers.

I remember garters, and combs stuck into the tops of long socks.

I remember M.E. Stores; woggles, sheath knives and broad-rimmed khaki scout hats with false leopard-skin hatbands.

I remember that Liberace had a costume fitted with epaulettes, electric lights and tassels that looked like the bottom of a theatre curtain.

I remember Ansteys, Stuttafords, John Orrs, Garlicks, Greatermans and Cleghorns in the middle of town; the haberdashery department, the lift-man on his seat and the lazy piano music in the tea-room on the top floor.

I remember Jeremy Taylor's song about the lift-girl who didn't even have time for a zizz (I thought that meant a pee).

I remember ladies standing around looking at dress patterns for hours.

I remember that you could take clothes home "on appro".

I remember capsules with shiny brass ends and a transparent middle, called "dockets", sent off with documents inside them and then arriving back via overhead tubes at the sales assistant's counter with a satisfying pop.

I remember the X-ray machine in shoe departments where you could look down through an eye-piece and see the bones of your feet inside a new shoe.

I remember the problem of tying your own shoe-laces. Girls didn't seem to have this problem because their shoe-laces never came undone.

I remember my grandmother's fear that I would get my shoe caught at the end of the escalator.

I remember tram-loads of old ladies on the way from Yeoville into town, and their fierce reaction if you accidentally trod on their feet.

I remember the red nail of a big toe pushing through the front of a woman's shoe like a tortoise-head.

I remember old ladies in fox-stoles with the dried head and paws still there.

I remember when a house down the road from my grandparents' was sealed for fumigation, and imagining processions of very small creatures heading for cover.

I remember my grandfather's wooden truncheon on his bedside table.

I remember pink electric blankets, and candlewick bedspreads with matching bedside mats.

I remember that my grandmother's gardener Willie festooned one of the outhouses with meat hanging from hooks to make biltong.

I remember my grandmother and her maid working at a chicken, the smell of fresh raw chicken-flesh rising up from the stone sink, and then the bitter whiff of singed feather stubs.

I remember my grandmother's mince machine with discs of different sized holes, and feeding in bread to force out the last of the meat.

I remember the Indian sammy coming around with his horse-drawn cart of fruit and vegetables.

I remember going to the Newtown fruit and vegetable market on Saturday mornings with my father; the auctioneers standing on ladders above bags and crates of fruit and vegetables, shouting a fast strange language that turned out to be prices.

I remember that I had to eat mangoes in the bath.

I remember going to a swimming pool at night to watch my plump uncles playing water-polo.

I remember the feeling of going hunting with my father when we examined all the things for sale at auction sales in private houses. And later the triumph of returning home to present my mother with the loot.

I remember mugs commemorating George V's visit to South Africa.

I remember:
     I'm the king of the castle,
     And you're the dirty rascal.

I remember being surprised to learn that the queen didn't wear her crown all day long.

I remember that I didn't go to school on the day South Africa became a republic, but the teacher kept a little flag and bronze medal for me anyway.

I remember not ever understanding the "ewegegebergtes" in *Die Stem*.

I remember singing hymns like:
>   All things bright and beautiful,
>   All creatures great and small.

and
>   Abide with me,
>   Fast falls the eventide,
>   The darkness deepens,
>   Lord with me abide.

I remember the big hushed sound of the whole school standing up or sitting down during assembly.

I remember the head boy at our high-school calling out: "School, rise!"

I remember that for punishment at high-school we had to stand outside the classroom getting bored and fearful in equal measure, hoping the ice-blue-eyed headmaster wouldn't come past.

I remember that when we dropped something our maths teacher asked us if we had the dropsy.

I remember him punishing us by smacking an open palm with a ruler while announcing: "Britannia rules the waves!"

I remember playing "Battleships".

I remember how to draw the figure ⬚ without lifting the pen from the page.

I remember log tables, in a little well-fingered book with a blue cover.

I remember boys using their watch-faces to deflect spots of sunlight across a class-room.

I remember little cut-out paper men attached by a thread to a spitball and flicked with a ruler to the ceiling of a class-room, where they hung for days on end like hopeless parachutists.

I remember questions like "Who wrote a book called 'I Fell Off a Cliff'?" (Answer: Eileen Dover.)

I remember a boy on the primary school coach trip to the Kruger National Park making up the first home-made love-song I had ever heard:
    I know a girl who's sweet as honey,
    I know a girl whose name's Leonie.

I remember a boy in the dormitory at the Kruger National Park who talked non-stop in his sleep, in a high-pitched girl's voice, with a vague smile on his lips.

I remember the joke about the boy who went to bed with a square root and woke up with a solution.

I remember the alleged game of "Splat", in which boys flicked jam against a bedroom wall using their erect penises, and the boy who flicked it highest won.

I remember a fancy-dress competition before a matinée performance at a cinema when one girl dressed up as a doll wrapped in cellophane.

I remember reaching the breathless moment in the middle of a film when I finally decided to grope for the hand of the girl I'd invited to come to the cinema precisely so I could reach that moment.

I remember:
    Gotta do ya bes' ta please her
    Jus' 'cos she's a livin' doll.

I remember The Shadows' hit single *Apache*, with *Needles of Penzance* on the flip side.

I remember listening to a song with lines that went something like:
    You get 'A' in Geography,
    You get 'B' in Zoology,
    You get 'C' in Biology,
    But you get 'D', 'D' in love.

I remember the exotic presence of girls at our high-school during sporting events.

I remember a handsome boy with his blonde student nurse girlfriend, out on the rugby field before a match.

I remember that not long afterwards he was killed in a car crash.

I remember I.Q. tests, and the teacher with the tic of shaking his head and blinking his eyes at the same time, who told me that with my I.Q. I should be doing *much* better at school.

I remember that for me learning Afrikaans was like trying to walk through a wall.

I remember tapped telephones.

I remember when you dialled a number and instead of the dialling tone you heard what was happening in the house at the other end, and wondered if one or both telephones were tapped.

I remember rare, dramatic overseas telephone calls.

I remember the cool weight of a black bakelite telephone.

I remember van Dyk floral carpets, passage runners, and telephone tables with blue and white Keren Kayemet collection boxes.

I remember my grandmother's telephone number: 43-3619.

I remember chocolate and ivory-coloured cameo brooches on the bosoms of older ladies.

I remember "Daisy, Daisy, give me your answer do", and white daisies with coat-button sized yellow centres.

I remember my grandmother dressed entirely in white next to my grandfather's van that had four flat tyres and was blocking the driveway.

I remember branches of pussy-willow in cut-glass vases.

I remember when Springbok Radio was never switched off.

I remember the gravelly voice advertising somebody or other's "Pine-tar and Honey"; "Eyes right with Eyegene"; and the moment when you could make out a few heavily accented English words on Radio Bantu, like "Black Cat Peanut Butter".

I remember *Forces Favourites*, with "min dae" included in all the messages.

I remember the Mark Saxon radio series, especially when he had to do battle with a creature from outer space that was trying to penetrate his brain.

I remember one of my uncles describing how he was on a bus eating peanut brittle when he suddenly discovered that there were worms in it.

I remember Crunchies, Flakey Bars, Peppermint Crisps, Chocolate Logs and sinking your teeth into the goo under the chocolate.

I remember Suchard Chocolate picture cards.

I remember taking the lining out of a cigarette box, peeling away the tissue paper, and smoothing the silver paper with the back of a spoon.

I remember packets of Lucky Strike white sugar cigarettes with red tips.

I remember epic visits to the dentist, whose name was Dr. Stoepel.

I remember how it felt to worry a loose milk-tooth with my tongue.

I remember paying a few pennies to sit on a bench in someone's garage and watch a puppet show, and another few pennies to buy an ice-cream sucker.

I remember when a puppeteer gave a jewelled umbrella brooch to the birthday girl during one of his puppet shows, and *I* wanted to be the one to give it to her.

I remember the "ice-cream boy" with his bell and three-wheeled bicycle, the vapours that rose up when he lifted the lid of the white ice-cream box, and rumours that his ice-cream could make you sick because he had already licked it.

I remember that if you press dry ice with a coin it squeaks.

I remember the Wall's ice-cream van with its out-of-tune recorded jingle.

I remember the "Dairy Den", "soft-serve" ice-cream with bits of nut or glacéd cherry extras, and the real Flakey you could get in the middle.

I remember "Sweet like a lemon in a storm breeze".

I remember Trini Lopez singing "Lemon tree very pretty" and "Green green".

I remember "Don't check me skeef, hey!"

I remember friends calling each other "my china".

I remember pictures of sullen Chinese miners in the Africana Museum, and a collection of ivory dice they used.

I remember "Ching Chong Cha": a fist for rock, two fingers for scissors and a palm for paper.

I remember Chinese bangle torture, diamond punches and paralysers.

I remember black maids waiting at the end of the street for the "fah fee man", who sometimes didn't come because of the police.

I remember seeing him one afternoon in his battered old American car, looking sallow and haggard.

I remember police raids in the middle of a weekday afternoon, black men running blindly for their lives, and hands against the grille at the back of the police-van.

I remember the police compound full of small, prefabricated houses, off Clarendon Circle below the Fort.

I remember that Special Branch men sat behind newspapers in Volkswagen Beetles by day, and in the branches of trees by night.

I remember the joke about two boys called Shut Up and Trouble who were playing hide-and-go seek. Shut Up couldn't find Trouble. Then a policeman asked him his name, and when he answered the policeman asked him if he was looking for Trouble.

I remember white policemen and Alsatians, and boys coming back from a football match repeating: "There wuz Alsaaaashunz."

I remember that Highlands Park was usually at the top of the white national soccer league.

I remember that feeling when we arrived to play football at a school we'd never been to before. Wondering how strong they were, if the field was bumpy, and what refreshments we would get.

I remember when Leicester City toured South Africa, and Gordon Banks was the goal-keeper.

I remember the dog-trainer with a padded arm who was pulled down to the ground by a leaping Alsatian during a dog-training demonstration at our primary school.

I remember the story of Sandra Laing whose skin was black though both her parents were white.

I remember the *With Love and Hisses* column by Molly Reinhardt in *The Sunday Times*, and *Stoep Talk* by Bob Connolly in *The Rand Daily Mail*.

I remember my father at a friends' house talking in an urgent hush about Sharpeville, and the peace and sunlight in the garden outside.

I remember the photos in the *Shooting at Sharpeville* book by Bishop Ambrose Reeves.

I remember that Prime Minister B.J.Vorster's idea was to make the cities of South Africa "white by night".

I remember the Immorality Act. And "miscegenation".

I remember " border industries".

I remember Chief Kaiser Matanzima, and one of the first stamps from the Transkei showing that there really was a parliament building there.

I remember when (black) garage attendants wore a silver change distributor like bus conductors.

I remember that black servants used to ask whites to bring them back bottles of sea-water from the coast, to use as an enema I think.

I remember the smooth metal capsules that were used to make soda water.

I remember rectangular red cold-drink fridges in garages, with bottles standing upright in the cold water: Coca-Cola, Pepsi-Cola, Fanta (orange, grape), and Hubbly Bubbly in bottles that looked as if they'd had chicken-pox.

I remember the congregation of children around garage fridges on Saturday afternoons, and the taste of a cold drink mixed with the smell of the oily garage floor.

I remember that there was "deposit" for a bottle.

I remember leaving a swimming pool and walking, barefoot and dripping wet down a hot tarred road to the garage to get a cold drink.

I remember that I thought Baden-Powell had something to do with B.P. petrol.

I remember scouts coming to our door to ask what they could do for "bob-a-job".

I remember how if you were obscuring the view of a boy sitting behind you at a sports' match he would say something like "Hey, is your old man a glass maker?" or "Hey, do you come from Glasgow?"

I remember that a friend of mine asked me for a sandwich while we were watching a swimming gala, took a bite and gave it back to me completely scandalized because there was meat and butter in it, so it wasn't kosher.

I remember my mother's sandwiches on long car rides, especially the ones with cream cheese and cucumber.

I remember asking my father to buy me kosher bacon.

I remember discovering Leo Rosten's *The Education of H*Y*M*A*N K*A*P*L*A*N* in a junk shop.

I remember that any way I considered the question, it was quite puzzling to be Jewish.

I remember that the best school fêtes were definitely at King David Primary School.

I remember finding a Playboy magazine at our primary school fête and being embarrassed to buy it, buying it anyway, and being overwhelmed by the naked women (one of them on all fours on a tiger-skin), who were looking at me personally.

I remember that when you went to a mixed party you were supposed to "get off with" a girl.

I remember "crushes", "getting fresh", "necking" and "going steady".

I remember shuffling around in a circle with a quite co-operative girl the first time I went to a mixed party, and then trying to work out what to do when the music stopped.

I remember the even bigger problem of what to do when the music slowed down because if you weren't ready to hold on to the girl you had been shuffling with, you had to abandon her and retreat to the wall.

I remember that sometimes there was "a lot of talent" at a party, and sometimes "the talent was lousy".

I remember boys in the bathroom combing their hair, already on the way to another party that no one else was supposed to know about.

I remember aluminium combs.

I remember being surprised to find that gate-crashers looked just like everyone else.

I remember stiff rounded collars with holes at their tips, and pins with a little screw-on top that linked them under the tie.

I remember pastel-coloured shirts with white turtle-necks underneath them.

I remember the glamour surrounding boys who played in bands at parties.

I remember Chubby Checker singing:
    Let's twist again,
    Like we did last summer.

I remember that Rhodesians had television. We had drive-ins.

I remember the melancholy atmosphere of drive-ins, everyone in a separate car on the same big tarmac with a film looming up out of the darkness.

I remember short loudspeaker poles lined up like a platoon in front of drive-in screens during the day.

I remember trying to imagine what it might feel like to be Helen Keller.

I remember little-finger-sized torches with fluorescent tips that were given to us one Christmas.

I remember going to the planetarium during the day and wondering, after a while, whether the night sky in there was real.

I remember wondering how God could be with people who were wide awake on one side of the world, and at the same time with the others who were fast asleep.

I remember waking up and seeing snow in Johannesburg for the first time in my life, and not realizing that it was snow.

I remember that the second time it snowed our high-school was invaded by boys from Helpmekaar Hoër Seunskool. We were let out of class to repel them with snow-balls.

I remember snowmen made of hail.

I remember watching little bits of snow waft down over a Christmas scene in a little plastic globe, and the need to shake it again.

I remember ballpoint pens you could tip up or down so that a boat or an aeroplane went sliding slowly along their length.

I remember shells that opened at the bottom of a glass of water, letting out a delicate paper flower on a thread.

I remember pink Nutty Putty in a plastic egg.

I remember Prince Valiant.

I remember my mother calling me "Sir Galahad" when she wanted to jolt me a little.

I remember a friend of mine who had a whole troop of lead soldiers.

I remember a friend of mine who had a steam-engine that puffed real steam.

I remember green metal Meccano sets.

I remember thick twisted silver wire circuits set up on a table at fêtes. There was a loop of thin wire you had to thread across the circuit without touching it, otherwise it buzzed.

I remember photographs in the paper showing quirky hobbies at the Hobbies Fair.

I remember the day we wanted to go to the Milner Park Fairground, but it was closed because Prime Minister J.G. Strydom had died.

I remember that Louis Trichardt travelled east and died of malaria.

I remember the lines across the map of South Africa, like trails of ants, one for each of the Great Trek leaders: Sarel Cilliers, Piet Retief, Potgieter, van Rensburg.

I remember that Paul Kruger lost a thumb.

I remember that trekker wives wore coal-shuttle hats.

I remember:
Janpierewit, Janpierewit,
Janpierewit staan stil,
Janpierewit, Janpierewit,
Janpierewit draai om.

Goeie môre my vrou,
Hiers 'n soentjie vir jou.
Goeie môre my man,
Daar is koffie in die kan.

I remember that when we went to the Africana Museum to have a look at a trekker wagon, one of the girls in our class had an epileptic fit; a teacher had to run off and find a spoon to stop her tongue from blocking her throat.

I remember snakes with wrinkled black and white paper skins and painted plaster heads suspended from a thread.

I remember that the blacks in our history textbooks usually had something to do with death.

I remember the unspeakable boredom of our van Jaarsveld history textbook.

I remember that someone important said something about "papering over the cracks". Maybe it was Bismarck speaking about the Congress of Vienna.

I remember the three brothers who were called on our primary-school intercom system because their father had died.

I remember the girl in our Standard Three class who accidentally dropped her brother from the balcony of their third floor flat.

I remember there was a bees' nest under the wing of the angel outside the War Museum.

I remember poppies with cloth petals on Poppy Day.

I remember feeling sorry for people who lived in flats.

I remember "flat-boys" in their night-blue-jean shirts and shorts with red piping, sometimes with checker-sized discs in their ear-lobes, and car-tyre sandals.

I remember reading a (banned) story about a black servant and his white madam making love, and wondering if things like that really happened.

I remember the commotion when a friend of mine returned from a stay overseas and was attracted by his family's young black maid.

I remember the Latin teacher at our school saying that dancing was "a navel battle without the semen."

I remember small black and white comic books about the Second World War or English soccer teams.

I remember cadets.

I remember spiffies and the problem of the collar shooting up while you were marching.

I remember garters, flashes, beret badges, and the sinking feeling when the effort to bone belts and boot-caps so they shone like glass failed so badly that they ended up looking more like skid-marks in mud.

I remember pressed uniforms and belts strapped to cake-tins being edged out of cars, followed by their anxious owners, on the day of the cadet competition.

I remember that it never rained on the day of the cadet competition.

I remember "short back and sides", and the ridicule heaped on any boy whose hair was considered to be too long.

I remember my father cheerfully saying "Don't shear him like a sheep" to the straight-faced barber upstairs at the O.K. Bazaars.

I remember the wooden board across the leather arms of the barber's chair; the cut-throat razor and the strop, the cold dab of Dettol-soaked cotton-wool. The dead silence.

I remember secretly shifting my hand under the sheet to get a lock of hair to roll onto the floor.

I remember crew cuts.

I remember white traffic-cops on big fast disgruntled motor-bikes, dressed in black uniforms with boots that hugged their calf muscles.

I remember that three friends of mine got a warning from a traffic-cop for jay walking.

I remember the man next door telling me that a gentleman always walks between a lady and the street.

I remember Abebe Bikila entering the Mexico City Olympic Stadium, barefoot.

I remember black and white Movietone news-reels at the cinema.

I remember black adults watching white schoolboy soccer matches from the fence on Riviera Road on a mid-week afternoon.

I remember pumping up the orange bladder of a football marked something like "Hand Sewn in Pakistan", and then the problem of tying the lace down so that there wasn't a bulge.

I remember the attraction of sleek, low-cut Adidas football boots.

I remember flying goalies.

I remember the difficulty of catching a medicine ball.

I remember blowing into an orange rubber balloon just before a hernia operation, and trying to crack a joke for all the masked people in the operating theatre just as they started fading away from me.

I remember the Bovril sandwich the night-nurse gave me in hospital. It was so disgusting that I stuffed it in the bottom section of my wooden pencil box.

I remember nail inspection at school, and the way you curled your fingers in to try and hide them if they weren't trim and pink.

I remember "For what we are about to receive may the Lord make us truly thankful", and the smell of sandwiches in wax-proof paper.

I remember "It's none of your beeswax!"

I remember "Ops us a sluk".

I remember that Hygiene was a separate subject.

I remember the moment when you bit into the jam of a jam doughnut.

I remember koeksisters, sticky fingers, and wondering who the sisters were.

I remember:
Sugar in the morning,
Sugar in the evening,
Sugar at supper time.

I remember Sports Day at primary school, rosettes and war cries, three-legged races (using school ties), potato-sack races, egg-and-spoon races, tug-of-war, girls with little bean-bags but I can't remember why, parents running barefoot in parent races.

I remember wondering how big people's feet got that way.

I remember the white thread of wool stretched across the field at the finishing line, and wondering what it would be like to win a race and break it.

I remember "Nix" and "Nikkies not on", with crossed fingers held up in the air; also, crossing your fingers behind your back hoping something wouldn't happen.

I remember " 'Strue's God".

I remember Red Rover, knifey-knifey, eggy ("Calling eggy number six"), and king stingers before school in the morning.

I remember when my front tooth was cracked by a cricket ball.

I remember *Stars of Tomorrow* on the radio, with Mrs. Egnos whose son Geoffrey was at our school.

I remember *Test the Team* on the radio, with Arthur Bleksley, Eric Rosenthal and Eric Walker.

I remember Miss South Africa beauty contests, with white finalists wearing one-piece swimming costumes and a sash showing the provinces they came from.

I remember the photo of Miss Holland on the front page of the newspaper when she became Miss World. My father thought she had a beautiful throat.

I remember the long shapely legs of Juliet Prowse.

I remember when it was in to wear mini-skirts.

I remember the little toy mirror you could shift in front of a plastic ballerina so that she did pirouettes.

I remember glass thermometers that snapped. And the cool feeling of a ball of mercury in the palm of the hand.

I remember spending a long time watching bubbles wobbling upwards in an aquarium.

I remember thermometers with red liquid in the big bulb at the bottom that you had to hold until the liquid bubbled and climbed up the shaft to show how passionate you were feeling.

I remember the little red cellophane fortune fish that told your fortune by the way it curled in the palm of your hand.

I remember balls of thin red writhing worms that you could buy for aquariums.

I remember the Yugoslav butchery in Braamfontein with rows of aquariums full of guppies and so many green plants they looked like liquid forests.

I remember the whining of the electric saw at the butchery, and the sawdust on the floor.

I remember a money-box at a butchery marked FOR OUR BOYS AT THE BORDER.

I remember when L.S.D. meant pounds, shillings and pence.

I remember that there was a protea on the tickey coin, sparrows on the farthing, a half-a-crown but not a crown, and the Queen's head on everything.

I remember that there were two rand in a pound; also that after one pound, two pounds, we had to get used to saying one rand, two *rand*.

I remember the bushels and stones, pecks, furlongs and hectares that kept cropping up in maths questions as if there weren't enough problems without them.

I remember the joke about little Johnny (in my father's jokes the boy was always called "little Johnny") who had forgotten his multiplication tables and could only remember the tune.

I remember our Afrikaans teacher saying: "Skryf dit op die tafel van jou hart, kêrel, skryf dit op die tafel van jou hart."

I remember *Die Huisgenoot*, *Scope*, *Personality*, and the breasts I used to hunt down in *Stern* magazine while waiting for my violin lesson.

I remember the despair of Burt Lancaster in *The Swimmer*.

I remember the moment in *Yellow Submarine* when a creature devours everything around it and then devours itself.

I remember boys going around singing "They call me mellow yellow."

I remember boys going around whistling the theme tune from *A Fistful of Dollars*.

I remember boys replying heatedly, at the slightest hint of a political question: "What would *you* do if a black man came to your door and he wanted to rape your wife and kill your children? Hey?"

I remember that when a group of us went out in various disguises onto the streets of Hillbrow and another group tried to find us, the three they missed completely were dressed as blacks, in straw hats and blue overalls, leaning against the fence of a building site.

I remember when Bram Fischer disappeared in the middle of Johannesburg and the police couldn't find him.

I remember wondering if he was in our neighbourhood, wanting to spot him and secretly do something for him.

I remember the press photos when he was arrested, showing how he had changed his face, and the headline saying he had been living under the name of Mr. Black.

I remember the theme song from *Z*, and the prosecutor with green-tinted glasses who wouldn't give up.

I remember:
    Ai zika zimba zimba zimba,
    Ai zika zimba zimba zee.
    Hold him down,you Zulu warrior,
    Hold him down, you Zulu chief chief chief chief.

I remember:
> Boom shacka lacka lacka,
> Boom shacka lacka lacka.

I remember songs on the coach taking our team to a rugby match, like:
> Hook-a chook-a my soda cracker,
> Does ya mama chaw tabbaca?

followed by terrible tales such as the one about a plane on fire, a parachute, a desert, camels and camel-shit, a beautiful woman with a tin chastity belt, and a can-opener.

I remember a song with a chorus that starts: "We're off to see the wild west sho-o-ow", and one of the verses about the Fakawi birds that fly and fly until they get totally lost and then exclaim: "Where the Fakawi? Where the Fakawi?"

I remember that moment in a rugby match when you saw one boy lying on the ground with his finger on the tip of an upright rugby ball waiting for a second boy to kick the ball over the posts, and you wondered what would happen if he missed.

I remember long white rugby boot laces that had to be tied behind and under the boot.

I remember the taste of orange slices at half-time.

I remember the "first reserve orange-peeler" insult.

I remember Dr. Danie Craven, Frik du Preez and the *Vat hom Fluffy!* song.

I remember the cheerleader down at the Wits swimming pool shouting out
    I put my finger in the woodpecker?s hole
    And the woodpecker said « Lord bless my soul!»
and then getting sections of the lunch-hour crowd to chant
    Take it out !
    Put it in !
    Take it out !

I remember that "to stinky" a girl meant to touch her sexual parts.

I remember "You're getting on my tits!" and "You little tit!"

I remember the competition for the top bunks in train compartments that were held up by a length of green leather as thick as a barber's strop.

I remember freshly formed temporary couples up there.

I remember:
    As djy kan vry soos ek kan vry
    Dan vry jy tot djy lekker kry
    Of kos yes! Oh yes of kos yes.

    Ooo, sakke sakke vol dagga,
    Kanne kanne vol wyn
    Tchetching tchetching,
    Djy is my meisie
    En ons ry nou op die trein.

I remember enamel mugs full of tepid water from the glass water cylinder at the end of the train corridor.

I remember the stillness and heat during the interminable stop at De Aar.

I remember the sound of men tapping train wheels, and the smirky joke about them being "tapologists".

I remember trying to mouthe the words of songs at Habonim camp, to hide the fact that I didn't know any Hebrew.

I remember the ring of boys and young men peeing on a fire at the end of the evening, and the nostril-biting odour of softly hissing logs.

I remember the holes in the fence around the girls' shower.

I remember breathless descriptions of girls' bodies that had been spied through those holes.

I remember wanting a girl and being afraid that she might respond, to the point of nausea.

I remember the question of what other people would think of the girl you had chosen.

I remember the question of girls remaining faithful to boys who hadn't come to camp with them.

I remember tinned curried fish, tinned sardines and oily chunks of Atlas bread.

I remember looking down the holes in the girls' toilet seats to the pit below, and coming to the conclusion that girls' turds were roundish; boys' turds were long.

I remember boys saying "I've got a shit on board."

I remember someone taking an eager swig from a Pepsi-Cola bottle that had been strategically placed at the middle of a trestle table before lunch at camp and then hurriedly spewing it out because it had been filled with Worcester sauce.

I remember:
> Close the doors, they're coming through the windows,
> Close the windows, they're coming through the doors;
> Close the doors, they're coming through the windows,
> Oh my gosh! They're coming through the floors!

I remember people saying that if it hadn't been for the blacks, the government would have turned on the Jews.

I remember wondering if Hitler really was dead.

I remember a photograph of Eichmann wearing thick black-rimmed spectacles and sitting in a glass box.

I remember the theme song from *Exodus*.

I remember a boy telling me that I obviously had enough money to be able to lend him some, because I was Jewish.

I remember Jewish boys crammed into a classroom listening to a transistor radio on the first day of the Six Day War.

I remember young Jewish men catching the plane for Israel during the Six Day War.

I remember the "Yeroushalayim shel zahar" song, and Dayan's eyepatch.

I remember pictures of Egyptian soldiers' boots lost in the desert.

I remember Leilah Khaled.

I remember the first time I felt like an emigrant: crossing a tarmac at night, in the dusty light of truck headlamps and the din of running motors, on arrival at an army camp in Kimberley.

I remember the second time: on emerging from the quartermaster-stores with army gear stacked so high against my stiff arms that I couldn't see where I was going.

I remember:
> This is your rifle and this is your gun,
> This is for shooting and this is for fun.

I remember soldiers sleeping on the cement floor next to their beds so they wouldn't have to make them at five o'clock the next morning.

I remember soldiers polishing brass-work in our bungalow at five o'clock the next morning.

I remember the Saturday night when officers had a party in our bungalow and made such a drunken mess of it we had to move out for a few days.

I remember "pull-through" for cleaning an F.N. rifle-barrel which, according to a knowledgeable corporal, looked as if an elephant had shat down it.

I remember one corporal's solution for acne pimples: "Skeer hulle af, kêrel."

I remember a talk against "kommunism" before the assembled troops one evening, illustrated by slides. One of them showed a statue of Marx, under-exposed so that it was almost entirely obliterated by darkness.

I remember "Jy raak wit!"

I remember leaving the army camp with other Jewish soldiers on a high holiday, and the whole rigmarole of having to say the right things to the members of the family who invited me into their Kimberley home to prove that I was at least as Jewish as they were.

I remember a soldier saying that masturbation was a good thing because "it cleans out the tubes."

I remember Kimberley root-beer in big green bottles.

I remember waiting for mail, particularly from one or two girls who I knew wouldn't send me any.

I remember the wall next to the three-tier bed-bunk in the deserted mine-compound where we were doing manoeuvres: right where the miner's head would have been as he fell asleep, glossy ads for necklaces, gold cigarette-lighters, smart cars.

I remember a soldier looking up at a low-flying aircraft and telling me there was no reason why anyone would want to drop a bomb on us.

I remember John Harris and the Park Station bomb.

I remember sitting in our school-bus on the day that John Harris was hanged, looking around at all the boys in their uniforms, trying to imagine him and them and me in the same country at the same time, and not managing.

I remember that John Harris went to the gallows chanting "We shall overcome."

I remember that the only thing I shared with boys at school about my father being in jail was the taboo of speaking about him.

I remember blank spaces in the newspaper and other publications to escape censorship.

I remember when black holes were discovered, and scientists going down into a mine to look for quarks.

I remember the trance of listening to the voice on the radio chanting stock-exchange figures.

I remember that just before the radio news there were a few high-pitched pips with a long one at the end.

I remember that children were sometimes buried alive when they went sliding down mine-dumps.

I remember that there were pot-holes after earthquakes on the Rand because of the dolomite.

I remember when one whole house with a family sleeping in it disappeared down a sinkhole.

I remember standing at the top of the tallest slide in the park with children lined up on the steps behind me, and whizzing down the strip of hot shiny metal.

I remember wondering what would happen if a person on one of those swings held by chains went over the top.

I remember when Gary Powers was shot down over the U.S.S.R.

I remember wondering about the pigs in the Bay of Pigs.

I remember Spiro Agnew.

I remember not understanding how Jack Ruby managed to shoot Lee Harvey Oswald if there were so many policemen around.

I remember that Lyndon B. Johnson's wife was called Ladybird.

I remember:
   Ladybird, Ladybird,
   Fly away home,
   Your house is on fire,
   Your children are gone.

I remember the joke about the drunk man who urinates into a toilet-bowl, reads "Shanks" and replies "It'sh a pleshure."

I remember when Franco Frescura had to apologise to B.J.Vorster after publishing a cartoon of his face at the bottom of a toilet–bowl in *Wits Student*.

I remember the crazy, nervous laughter in the *Goon Show*.

I remember Tweetiebird saying "I taut I taw a putty tat."

I remember Elmer Fudd and his carrot patch.

I remember Archie and Veronica and one of their friends called Jughead.

I remember the columns of little black mail-order ads at the end of the comic book, especially one for body building equipment that showed a muscular man kicking sand in the face of a puny one.

I remember the cheap desolation of photo comics.

I remember sitting in a room with lace curtains at my grandmother's house reading comics till my mind went numb.

I remember boxes of empty Purity baby-food jars outside our kitchen door.

I remember the Stork Nappy Service.

I remember "Don't catch a nappy rash."

I remember the same dog-eared book by Dr. Spock in every house where there was a baby.

I remember that our washing machine had a mangle.

I remember big safety pins with pastel-coloured shifting safety heads.

I remember the tinkle of several glass baby bottles being boiled together in a pot.

I remember my father showing me how to blow bubbles from a film of soap between the thumb and forefinger.

I remember the suffering of the fat boy in our Standard Four class, especially during swimming period when his breasts were exposed.

I remember swimming costumes rolled up in towels in special plastic-lined swimming bags.

I remember boys flicking their towels at each other in the change-rooms.

I remember how we had to hold onto the side of the swimming pool and kick up the water till it frothed "like ice-cream".

I remember that our class won an ice-cream cake after we brought in the highest number of old newspapers from home.

I remember the first conscious lie I told my parents, about stealing a slab of chocolate from the kitchen dresser (there were no other possible culprits).

I remember repainting the kitchen dresser out in the garden with my father, and sunlight glistening on fresh cucumber-green paint.

I remember helping our neighbour to wash out her son's mouth with soap after he had lied.

I remember children going to elocution lessons.

I remember Royal Instant Chocolate Pudding and Royal Instant Butterscotch Pudding, and drawing slow basket-weaving designs with my spoon against the bottom of my bowl while the adults went on talking.

I remember licking the pot.

I remember the trifle my mother made for birthdays (with Boudoir biscuits, a dash of rum, sliced up jelly, whipped cream and hundreds and thousands); her squeaky cellophane bags of sweets, and jelly in frilly pleated paper bowls.

I remember banana slices in jelly.

I remember five or six hypnotised volunteers up on a stage in Hermanus who were each given a potato, and told it was an apple. They all chewed it down to the core, then spat out what was left in their mouths when they were brought round.

I remember wondering how far a hypnotist could go if he desired one of his subjects.

I remember that our history teacher was rumoured to have only one breast.

I remember an Afrikaans story we had to read about a woman who kept having the same dream about living a few centuries back in an ancestral castle in Holland.

I remember waking up with an arm so thick and numb that it felt as if I wouldn't be able to use it again.

I remember the hypnotic comfort of lying in bed describing a figure eight with my toes across the inside of the top sheet.

I remember staying in bed the whole day when I was ill, sounds of the maid in the house, peace and light in the garden past the insect-netting on the windows, and mid-morning virile voices on the radio meant for bored housewives.

I remember doing jigsaw puzzles on a tray in bed.

I remember our family doctor taking throat-swabs. He used cotton wool at the end of a length of wire, fixed to the cork of a test-tube.

I remember Sucrets, for sucking when you had a sore throat, that made the tongue go numb.

I remember Mylol against mosquitoes, crushed pills mixed into All Gold fig jam, and Calamine lotion dabbed onto itchy bites.

I remember sleeping-bag feathers all over a tent one morning after a hopeless, epic battle against mosquitoes.

I remember D.H. Lawrence's poem about a mosquito, and the one about the snake that came to his drinking hole.

I remember skipping pages of *Lady Chatterley's Lover* to get to the sexy parts, when the gardener addresses his lover as "thee" and says things to her like "Come to me."

I remember trying the "Come to me" part with a girl. It sounded all wrong.

I remember the school-boy who stole condoms from the back of a Volkswagen parked outside our house.

I remember that, from a distance, condom tins looked like snuff tins.

I remember the rumour that the VW on the Volkswagen Beetle would turn into a swastika at a certain speed.

I remember hitch-hiking a ride in a Volkswagen Beetle with three Afrikaners who went cruising slowly past farmland on the lookout for "kaffir-girls".

I remember hitch-hiking a ride with a man who assured me that blacks had "just had their tails cut off". He invited me into his home to meet his family.

I remember that he had a giant picture of Raquel Welch with her breasts pressing out of an animal-skin bikini top, against the orange wall behind the bar in his living room. Next morning his young daughter brought me breakfast in bed.

I remember that when you were hitchhiking, the drivers who couldn't give you a lift were always the ones with the warmest smiles.

I remember the way Peter Fonda and Dennis Hopper leaned back in their bikes in *Easy Rider*.

I remember when I discovered that the words of one of the songs in *Hair* were taken from *Hamlet*.

I remember:
    Jesus Christ, Superstar,
    Who in the world do you think you are?

I remember how Goldreich and Wolpe escaped across the border disguised as priests.

I remember that I didn't ever see a map of the African continent hung up in a classroom.

I remember the diplomatic "triumph" of B.J.Vorster meeting Houphouet-Boigny of the Ivory Coast, and a photo of them in the paper wearing tuxedos and smiling.

I remember how photographers would take your portrait while you were walking through the streets in the middle of Johannesburg, and then come up to you and hand you their card.

I remember the problem of loading a Brownie camera.

I remember when *The Family of Man* exhibition came to Johannesburg.

I remember the bright cartoon-style maps of South Africa on the back of Post Toastie boxes.

I remember off-white little plastic birds and animals you could get from the garage in exchange for a certain number of bottle tops, and the cardboard wall-map of South Africa you could slot them into.

I remember when bottle tops were lined with cork.

I remember the noise of a stiff, bent, yellowish waxed paper straw when you were trying to suck up what was left of a milk shake.

I remember being told to mind my p's and q's, and trying to work out what the q's were.

I remember trying to work out the meaning of expressions like "You can't have your cake and eat it too" (How could you possibly eat the cake if you didn't have any in the first place?)

I remember our maths teacher explaining infinity to us: you can go on taking no marbles out of a bag forever.

I remember that parallel lines only meet at infinity.

I remember those little arrows you had to draw on lines in geometry diagrams to show that they were parallel.

I remember pea-shooters with canna seeds for ammunition, and "catties" with stiff varnished wire handles.

I remember Davy Crockett racoon-tail caps, and:
Davy, Davy Crockett,
King of the wild frontier.

I remember using a long stick to fish out feathers from the bird-cages at the zoo. Especially peacock feathers.

I remember speculation about the length of Errol Flynn's member. I had no idea *who* Errol Flynn was; his member had an entirely independent existence.

I remember the spectacular kick to the crotch in *Butch Cassidy and the Sun-Dance Kid*.

I remember a boy holding a small audience in the corridor before class began, talking about a girl's "quam" that was so big you could fit a milk-bottle into it.

I remember that a bird used to peck through the lids of milk-bottles on our stoep.

I remember chips of ice in the cream at the top of milk-bottles on winter mornings.

I remember organising races between rain-drops, then watching to see which one reached the bottom of the window-pane first.

I remember the magnetic attraction between puddles and galoshes.

I remember imagining what it would be like if it just didn't stop raining and our whole neighbourhood was washed away.

I remember water restrictions during periods of drought, including the encouragement to use the same bath-water twice.

I remember the cool oozy feel of the mud roads I made at the side of our driveway.

I remember Matchbox cars and Dinky toys.

I remember that "Made in Hong Kong" meant bad quality.

I remember Morris Minors, hump-backed little Fiats, and Ford Anglias with tail lights pointed like varnished fingernails.

I remember lots of tank-sized, oil-blue Mercedes Benzes driving around Johannesburg, and boys dreaming of Ford Mustangs and Porsches.

I remember sentences beginning: "Meanwhile, back at the ranch ...".

I remember that when my father first bought a car, my mother didn't believe he'd finally done it, and went all around the house looking for the real owner.

I remember sitting sleepily in the back of our car at night, hypnotised by the flash of cats-eyes down the middle of the road.

I remember boys going around saying: "E-e-everybody into my poliesie-van!"

I remember the broken telephone joke my father told me. It began "We're going to advance, lend us reinforcements," and ended "We're going to a dance, lend us three and fourpence."

I remember those telephones we used to play with, made of two jam tins connected by a long piece of string knotted to each base.

I remember ex-servicemen.

I remember a man referring with awe to *When Smuts Goes* by Arthur Keppel-Jones, as if South Africa's destiny had already been pre-recorded there.

I remember that our English teacher was rumoured to have an iron lung after fighting in the war. Maybe that was why he murmured "errr" after he'd finished speaking.

I remember my aunt Tybie coming over to me during my grandmother's funeral and softly saying something like "Iyishoo Ongife," which I thought must be one more Yiddish or Hebrew expression I couldn't understand. I said it back to her even more softly, and as accurately as possible.

I remember that a few years later I heard the same thing but a bit more clearly: "I wish you a long life."

I remember a man coming to our high-school to warn us about the dangers of smoking. The "unhealthy" lung he showed us was almost black. But the "healthy" one was ash-grey and even uglier.

I remember Life cigarettes.

I remember the proud sullen atmosphere at "Smoker's Corner" during break, on the rugby field furthest from the school buildings.

I remember fights after school, down below the main classrooms at the "Cabbage Patch".

I remember bent, nicotine-stained pipe-cleaners in ash-trays.

I remember that you can dab nicotine onto cacti as a remedy against some kind of fungus.

I remember that school-girls never seemed to smoke.

I remember kugels.

I remember realising that beauty spots weren't necessarily real, and wondering what else wasn't.

I remember Tretchikoff's paintings of roses, with dewdrops on the petals.

I remember The Singing Nuns and "Domini-que, ni-que, ni-que".

I remember black mourning bands on jacket arms.

I remember black men wearing brown hats with a little guinea-fowl feather in the hat-band.

I remember white men wearing grey hats, and men in houses with the mark of a hat-rim still lightly grooved at their temples.

I remember bicycle clips on flannel trousers with turn-ups.

I remember playing cards pegged to bicycles so that they made a whirring sound like a trapped bird against the wheel-spokes.

I remember stiff leather bicycle saddles with a tennis ball wedged between the springs.

I remember the click and wheeze of our maid's primus stove being primed. And mealie-pap with Irish stew in a chipped enamel plate.

I remember the cheap dusty whiff of the Players' cigarettes she used to smoke.

I remember a kitchen with a formica table and chairs. Overhead, a green metal lamp-shade with a pulley, and a long yellowish twist of fly paper stuck with flies.

I remember budgies in cages with millet sticks, cuttlefish, little round mirrors and bells.

I remember *The Birdman of Alcatraz.*

I remember the troubles in Attica prison.

I remember Angela Davis and Afro hairstyles.

I remember when young black men in Johannesburg started growing their hair and wearing Black Power T-shirts.

I remember when it was in to greet people with a "black" hand-shake, and the moment of hesitation when the other person wasn't going through the same motions as you.

I remember when it was in to take Zulu 1 at Wits.

I remember that iskwikiskwiki is a Zulu name for a new shoe that squeaks.

I remember Winston Ntshona in *Sizwe Banzi is Dead*, consuming an orange with juice dripping from his chin as he thinks about the woman he has just met in a shebeen.

I remember Albee's *The Death of Bessie Smith*, with the man on the telephone crying "But I've got a woman in there" as he tries to get an ambulance; and Barney Simon clicking his fingers as the dialogue switched from character to character during his production at The Bantu Men's Social Centre in Dorkay House.

I remember the moment of unspoken tension after a theatre performance when the blacks went back to the townships and the whites went off to the suburbs.

I remember hitch-hiking a ride across the Karoo in a very warm truck with two black drivers who asked me to take over so that they could sleep.

I remember hitch-hiking a ride in a yellow Volvo with two whites who had drugged themselves to the gills. They also asked me to take over.

I remember Donovan singing:
    Yellow is the colour of my true love's hair
    In the morning, when we rise.

I remember the Rolling Stones singing "She's like a rainbow."

I remember Leonard Cohen singing "Your hair upon the pillow like a sleepy golden storm."

I remember fancy new Crayola wax crayons in an upright box (orange with green lettering) of several tiers including silver, gold and copper. There was also a wax-crayon sharpener fitted into the side of the box.

I remember Derwent pencil crayons whose tips melted into paint when you dipped them in water.

I remember indelible pencils, and the thread of purplish-blue in your saliva if you licked them.

I remember fringing a map with a blue crayon and then smudging it outwards with a tissue to make the sea.

I remember the dark amber swirl of whole-grape jam in my grandmother's tea.

I remember pricking my finger and then looking at the blood under a toy microscope with a real built-in light shining from below onto the slide.

I remember a South African stamp with a bright little orange tree that I asked my grandfather to tear off all his old envelopes for me.

I remember the yellowish false-looking colour of the first one cent pieces, with a Voortrekker wagon on one side.

I remember the way the image appeared when you did a pencil rubbing of a coin on tracing paper.

I remember "painting by numbers" oil paintings on living-room walls.

I remember learning from Mr. Saunders in Standard Four how to paint jacaranda trees using purple water-colours sprinkled with dry white paint powder.

I remember the earthy smell of paint powder mixed into a paste.

I remember the smell of freshly printed purple roneo-machine pages that we stuck into exercise books, and the factory noise of the roneo machine.

I remember the teacher pressing a rubber stamp onto a page of our exercise books after stabbing it into a purple ink-pad.

I remember that the Phoenicians traded in purple dye that came from bluebottles.

I remember the film about Old Yellow.

I remember the yellow-green mango-chutney my mother's grateful coloured patients gave her, and how it started a fire in your mouth.

I remember when Japanese people suddenly became "honorary whites" after they started trading in steel with South Africa.

I remember when Dag Hammarskjöld died in a plane crash. I think his successor was U Thant.

I remember that Chief Albert Luthuli was supposed to have been accidentally killed by a train.

I remember that Dr. Hastings Banda walked all the way to South Africa to study.

I remember Tanganyika, Basutoland and Bechuanaland, Northern and Southern Rhodesia and Nyasaland.

I remember how large Joshua Nkomo looked in newspaper photos.

I remember The Gold Coast.

I remember imagining Dr. Albert Schweitzer in a big airy house at the end of a forest with crowds of lepers crawling around outside.

I remember that Zanzibar was full of cloves.

I remember big bins for flour and sugar in the pantry.

I remember when toasters had metal flaps that opened out on both sides.

I remember when sheets had to be sprinkled with water before they were ironed, and the smell of steam puffing out of them.

I remember the whole palaver of defreezing the fridge.

I remember cylindrical yellow boxes of Vim scouring powder.

I remember maids sitting on the back lawn with their legs straight out in front of them polishing the silverware with Silvo.

I remember cheese and tomato jaffles, and the smell of melted cheese dripping onto a hot-plate.

I remember jars of orange-coloured cheese-spread with a nice sweet chemical taste.

I remember the danger of half a soggy Marie biscuit slipping into the tea.

I remember hot Milo or cocoa milk drinks at bed-time, with a wrinkled milk skin at the top of the mug.

I remember that the only alcohol we had in our house was "cooking wine".

I remember that I thought "a Martini on the rocks" meant you went out onto the rocks to drink it.

I remember black men coming out of Bennie Goldberg's Bottle Store with brown paper bags, and tipping the bottle to their mouths without removing the bag.

I remember demijohns of Lieberstein sparkling white wine.

I remember when it was in for whites to jive at parties.

I remember Wopko Jensma dancing like an owl with his thick-rimmed glasses on, hopping from one foot to the other.

I remember when Johnny Clegg brought a sizeable group of young black men to dance in the Women's Common Room on the first floor of the Wits Student Union building, and the whole place started shaking.

I remember Sunday afternoon at Wits, sunlight on car roofs, glossy purple ranunculi, occasional yelps from the swimming pool, and the pulse of live black jazz.

I remember the way Dollar Brand *concentrated*.

I remember Headquarters in Cape Town, The Troubadour in Johannesburg, and Mike Dickman singing:
> Down the road,
> down the road,
> heavy work for a
> horny toad.

I remember when girls wore boots with leather thong laces that wound all the way up their thighs.

I remember fringes of leather across suede jackets, long hair and fuzzy side-burns below the ear-lobe.

I remember the bus in *The Electric Kool-Aid Acid Test*.

I remember packets of Kool-Aid, with a picture of a cold glass on which a happy face was streaming with drops of condensed water.

I remember Lecol, and the little man on Oros orange juice bottles.

I remember the boy who called me "Oom" when I was walking down the road in Melville. He wanted to sell me a Benson and Hedges box full of loquats.

I remember Afrikaans children walking barefoot along the street.

I remember other children shouting out "Afrikaner vrot banana."

I remember the stiff defiant look on children's faces when they said "Sticks and stones can hurt my bones, but words can never hurt me," and you knew they were hurt.

I remember when all the election posters showed pictures of white men, apart from Helen Suzman.

I remember when Helen Joseph was under house arrest.

I remember women from The Black Sash standing on a traffic island outside Wits University.

I remember white women going to jail for short periods after refusing to pay fines for having blacks without passes staying on their property.

I remember finding myself in one of those women's mansions one night, and realising with some apprehension that her husband wasn't coming home.

I remember the cover of Germaine Greer's *The Female Eunuch*: a ready-to-wear woman's torso with handles at the hips.

I remember sweaty clothes, jock-straps and Wintergreen in the change-rooms after a rugby match.

I remember the catastrophe of our matric dance. The way the girl I had invited wore a prim dress that made her look like somebody's mother. The insect-repellent smell of her bee-hive hair-do. The dance floor like glue on my shoes.

I remember the pit in my stomach when I learnt that she had invited someone else to *her* matric dance.

I remember the association game when one boy said "Hazel" with a dreamy smile every time it was his turn because he could associate her with just about anything.

I remember:
> Don't cry on my shoulder,
> Rely on someone who's older,
> I don't know what to tell you
> When you ask about lo-o-o-o-ove.

I remember that boys got acne. Girls got periods.

I remember bits of Band Aid on popped acne pimples.

I remember our maid working at her corns with a Gillette's safety razor blade.

I remember the smell of my father's Prel shaving cream.

I remember the twitch of my father's moustache – seen from below – while he was trimming it.

I remember the chemical smell and greasy touch of long bars of blue-veined carbolic soap.

I remember the darkness of trading stores in the middle of the day.

I remember the collection of brittle grey dead objects in the windows of "witchdoctor shops".

I remember when whites had books by Credo Mutwa on their coffee tables, with pictures of him wearing animal skins and throwing bones.

I remember John Blacking beating out Venda drum rhythms on his lectern during anthropology lectures.

I remember people listening to the Missa Luba after it was used in *If* ...

I remember going to the cinema and wondering which parts the censors had cut.

I remember the sneaking suspicion that if the censors had passed a film it might just not be worth going to see.

I remember the tension at passport control when you wondered what the officer with the inscrutable look on his face could read next to your name, and then at customs when you wondered what was going to be confiscated.

I remember that my father managed to get hold of Eldridge Cleaver's *Soul on Ice* in jail.

I remember dreaming of my father escaping from jail and pitching up at the front door during the Pesach dinner at his parent's house.

I remember the only thing my father told me about his grandmother: she said you mustn't eat standing up, otherwise the food goes into your feet.

I remember that one of my aunts had a particular liking for chicken neck.

I remember gefilte fish, snoek, chopped liver sprinkled with chopped hard-boiled egg, chopped herring, and tongue.

I remember all the glowing bell-jars of stewed peaches and apricots stored in my grandmother's pantry.

I remember standing in there, sticking a peppercorn up my nostril and not being able to get it out.

I remember the desolate rectangle of my grandmother's back-yard.

I remember my uncles spitting apricot pips onto the corrugated iron roof of the house next door.

I remember the wall along my grandmother's neighbour's driveway, with broken glass stuck in cement at the top

I remember the strawberry milk-shake liquid in a bottle with a double curve that my grandmother used to buy me.

I remember how often you used to hear or read about women's breast, hip and waist measurements, and that the ideal figure was 36-24-36.

I remember when women's underwear was called "foundation garments".

I remember petticoats. And girdles.

I remember slacks.

I remember when women were "the weaker sex".

I remember imagining *The Titanic* going down, with women and children in lifeboats being lowered into the sea while the men stood calmly and heroically on deck.

I remember secretly paging through my mother's thick anatomy books to have a good look at all the awful things that could happen to the human body.

I remember standing in the change-room just before swimming period at primary school, looking at other boys' bodies and convincing myself I had a terminal illness which no one was telling me about.

I remember ladders in navy blue school tights.

I remember girls handpicking the boys who could write in their little pastel-paged autograph albums, and then going around showing other girls what had been written.

I remember some of the entries, including one about an elephant crossing the grass that ended: "now don't be mistaken and don't be misled, that little elephant slipped on his head". Another one was "G.U.R.A.Q.T.".

I remember autographs all over plaster casts.

I remember a production of *The Pied Piper of Hamelin* during a primary school concert when one of the rats fell off the stage.

I remember Des Lindbergh and Dawn Silver singing songs like "There's a hole in my bucket"; "A long time ago when the earth was green"; and "It's a hot and a heavy load, and a long and a dusty road".

I remember Keith Blundell singing:
  I can't hear a word
  I've got beans in my ears.

I remember reproductions of old blue Dutch tiles on plasticised kitchen wall-paper.

I remember the spittoons in Simon van der Stel's house.

I remember how black men would suddenly start polishing slowly when you walked into a museum.

I remember The East African Pavilion, where waiters wore a red sash and a fez, and I think the floorboards creaked.

I remember tea-time with my grandmother and great-aunt, in the tea-room at the Zoo, or places like The Balalaika somewhere in the northern suburbs. Especially the warm scones with melted butter, strawberry jam and a dollop of cream.

I remember hand-knitted tea cosies.

I remember the chewy part after you ate a meringue.

I remember when there was a competition to find a name for a new administrative district including Sandown and Bryanston. I couldn't believe anybody would pick the dead weight of a name like "Sandton".

I remember lift-schemes, and how other boys' mothers always seemed to have the time to participate in them.

I remember that you almost never saw a taxi in the suburbs of Johannesburg, and that virtually the only blacks who drove through there in cars were chauffeurs.

I remember that to travel the 400 miles from Johannesburg to Durban in our Morris Minor, we left at first light and arrived well after dark.

I remember looking for a "travelling companion" – a car travelling as slowly as we were. None of them ever lasted very long.

I remember playing the number plate game.

I remember number plates beginning with the letters T.J., T.A. (Benoni), T.B. (Boksburg), T.K., T.P., T.S., T.V. (Vereeniging), T.V.B. (Vanderbijlpark), O.B., C.A., N.D., N.P. (Pietermaritzburg) and N.P.N. (Pinetown), as well as G.G. (Government Garage) which was sometimes written in red.

I remember the buzz of rivalry around the motorbike shed at our high-school.

I remember Stirling Moss.

I remember that the man in *A Man and a Woman* was a racing driver, and the woman was Anouk Aimée. When you started humming the theme song you couldn't stop.

I remember our pet tortoise, and its sorry end.

I remember we inherited a black dog called Chaka who died of sadness.

I remember that our cat went crazy.

I remember Gerald Durrell's *My Family and Other Animals*.

I remember my grandfather's stained dark wooden dog clock with hours in one eye and minutes in the other. It sat on a doily and never worked.

I remember the three monkeys on the mantelpiece: See no evil, Hear no evil and Speak no evil. Also, small ebony elephants with ivory tusks.

I remember big sepia wedding photographs standing on the floor next to the sideboard where the playing cards were kept.

I remember a song about someone's grandfather's clock that
Stopped, short, never to go again,
When the old man died.

I remember the egg-shaped steel-grey pellets of coke my grandmother used in her stove.

I remember heaters disguised as plastic fire-places.

I remember that some people made real log fires on Christmas day, even if the sun was beating down outside.

I remember blacks shouting out "Happy! Happy!" in the street at Christmas time.

I remember that I thought Boxing Day had something to do with boxing.

I remember trying to work out the reason for the spelling of "Xmas", and coming to the conclusion that if you said "Crossmas" fast enough, it turned into "Christmas".

I remember black men drinking from plastic bottles of horribly blue methylated spirits.

I remember black boys sniffing aeroplane glue on the square outside the Johannesburg Library.

I remember stopping my car some fifty yards before a red light on Jan Smuts Avenue, with no cars ahead of me (and several behind), while enjoying the delayed effects of a grass cookie.

I remember Bob Dylan singing "Meantime life outside goes on all around you."

I remember a packed showing of *Don't Look Back* in someone's living room in Parkview.

I remember the sound of the flute in music by Jethro Tull.

I remember *Disraeli Gears* by The Cream.

I remember the song by The Traffic about John Barleycorn.

I remember people who always knew a rock band that was better than the one you enjoyed listening to.

I remember when it was in to wear purple.

I remember cork platform shoes, velvet bags with sequins, sunglasses and Chiclets.

I remember young women with short hair in hotpants.

I remember young men with long sideburns in bell-bottoms. Also, floral shirts with long pointed collars, and neck-chains.

I remember *Music to Watch Girls By*.

I remember *Tubular Bells*.

I remember "the wet look".

I remember Twiggy.

I remember "progressive dinners".

I remember drive-in dinners at The Doll House.

I remember my mother's strained red borscht, with hot potatoes, slices of hard-boiled egg and cucumber, and a dollop of cream, all going red at the edges.

I remember the blotted colours of *The Rand Daily Mail* front page photographs showing the best garden of the month, or pretty girls.

I remember Bob Connolly's *Breakfast Quip*.

I remember the first front page headlines about suspect deaths in prison, and then more of them.

I remember Ahmed Timol.

I remember Jock Strachan's articles in *The Rand Daily Mail* about conditions for white male political prisoners.

I remember a story about Houdini being chained and thrown into a river covered with ice. He was supposed to have discovered he could breathe thanks to a thin layer of air between the ice and the water, while he picked the lock.

I remember falling into a pond at The Wilds while scooping tadpoles off the side in a cardboard cup.

I remember the squelch of wet leather sandals.

I remember a Little Golden Book about the four seasons in the United States, showing pictures of children splashing around in spurts of water from a fire hydrant, and in thin jets of water streaming from the back of a truck.

I remember:
    Cowboys and crooks,
    Pull down your broeks!

I remember "I wrote a letter to my love and on the way I dropped it", and feeling with your hand to check whether the letter had been dropped behind your back.

I remember that the first story I wrote, on a few small pages stapled together, was called *Rufus the Rabbit*, and the small hoarse laugh of Rufus's mother when I proudly handed it to her.

I remember when we were all practising our signatures.

I remember counting the words in compositions with titles like "My summer holiday" and "A day in the life of a tickey", and never having enough to say.

I remember that dassies belong to the same family as elephants.

I remember that female praying mantises eat their mates.

I remember a joke, somehow connected with the Kinsey report, that some people believed "homosexual" meant you did it at home, and "auto-erotic" meant it happened in a car.

I remember jokes that began "To the woods, to the woods".

I remember:
    Roll me over in the clover,
    Roll me over, lay me down and do it again.

I remember that you have to roll someone who is on fire in a blanket or a carpet.

I remember heaters made of a rectangular greyish asbestos.

I remember learning about "the kiss of life" at high and fantasies of having to use it to save the lives of two girls in particular.

I remember the question of how to count freck especially when they overlapped.

I remember when boys first started peroxiding their hair.

I remember jeans with streaks and blotches of bleach across them.

I remember white canvas takkies, with a rubber toecap and a flat rubber sole.

I remember paint-sized tins of Cobra and Sunbeam polish for stoeps.

I remember pogo sticks, and Pogo comics.

I remember Hush Puppies.

I remember brown or beige corduroy jackets, velskoene and beards.

I remember "We are marching to Pretoria", "Vat jou goed en trek Ferreira", "It's a long way to Tipperary", and "Pack up your troubles in your old kit bag and smile, smile, smile".

I remember the whistling in *Bridge Over the River Kwai*.

I remember that the remotest place in the world was Timbuktu.

I remember that England was six thousand miles away, but Europe seemed much further.

I remember learning the expression "going to the dogs" from my great aunt Essie, who said that England was going there.

I remember a man telling me that if you were bored with London you were bored with life.

I remember French letters, the French kiss, French leave, French cricket (with a tomato crate), French knitting and French toast.

I remember pouring plaster of Paris into upside-down red rubber moulds (one was of a pride of lions) suspended in jars or holes cut into the base of shoe-boxes.

I remember that the first time I was taken to the theatre I saw a play about a boy who had a magical pair of scissors: whatever he cut out of the air turned into something real.

I remember toy drums with stretched reddish rubber skins, and toy silver trumpets which came with little scores for tunes like "Come to the cook house call, boys".

I remember my gramophone. You wound it up with a crank, and twisted half the shiny tubular arm upwards to put in a new steel needle from a little metal dish.

I remember 78s, seven singles, 45s and L.Ps.

I remember a boy playing a song that began "My old man's a dustman" on a small pale blue plastic guitar for the whole class in Standard Two.

I remember being in the orchestra that did a rendering of Hayden's *Toy Symphony* under the direction of my music teacher, Miss Ilse von Pfluck-Hartung. I played the triangle.

I remember Miss von Pfluck-Hartung's music studio, with its heavy smell of dog meat, poodle pee, and Johnson and Johnson's Baby Powder.

I remember Baby Shows.

I remember the sounds in our house on the night that my mother was driven off by my father to give birth to my brother.

I remember discovering the owner of our house nailing a "For Sale" sign onto a tree outside our house one weekend, without bothering to tell us beforehand that we were going to have to move out.

I remember when the owner of our house came and stole my father's succulent and cacti collection from the rockery just before we moved out.

I remember sitting in our hot car, watching as my mother emerged triumphantly from a Houghton mansion, with my father behind her bearing a couple of tomato crates piled with our plants.

I remember that the father of a boy at our school escaped death because a bullet from the gun he was cleaning glanced off the packet of cigarettes in his chest pocket.

I remember the complicity between some fathers and our headmaster, especially while watching school rugby matches.

I remember when I almost set fire to our house by burning a pile of twigs and grass under a dry bush next to the kitchen with a magnifying glass.

I remember Bunsen burners.

I remember our chaotic, fast-speaking science teacher whose experiments always seemed to be on the point of exploding.

I remember the dry sound of our maid chopping up pinewood logs for the fire.

I remember black road-gangs singing as they swung picks against the road, and the boss sitting silently in the shade.

I remember that sharpened bicycle spokes were used as deadly weapons in the township.

I remember black plastic-handled knives with screw-in side-shafts to regulate the thickness of a slice of bread.

I remember that on Thursdays restaurants like The Golden Spur were packed with families at dinner-time because it was the maid's day off.

I remember my mother's fury when I refused to eat meat any more.

I remember headbands, sandalwood bracelets, bushy beards, musk perfume and kundalini.

I remember The Incredible String Band.

I remember *Siddhartha* by Herman Hesse.

I remember Baba Ram Dass.

I remember when the Little Guru came to South Africa, and all his followers had the same vision of something multi-coloured in the sky.

I remember the pretty girl who read to me from one of those slim quote-books of universal wisdom that love is not looking at someone but looking with someone in the same direction.

I remember problems between a yoga teacher and one or two women who weren't as attracted to him as he had imagined.

I remember Carole King singing:
  Winter, spring, summer or fall,
  All you've gotta do-o is ca-a-all
  And I'll come ru-unning."

I remember when everyone was reading Khalil Gibran's *The Prophet*.

I remember when everyone was reading *Jonathan Livingstone Seagull.*

I remember rumours about the Maharishi, The Beatles and Mia Farrow.

I remember people with illuminated faces saying "Shooh!" and describing the colours they saw when meditation took them up the chakras.

I remember when some of my friends had been arrested, and others were doing headstands with me during a yoga class.

I remember *Music For Zen Meditation.*

I remember pictures in the paper of Buddhist monks in Vietnam sitting with their robes on fire in public places.

I remember the two noises when a needle skidded from the end of the last track across the smooth vinyl at the end of a record and then against the paper label.

I remember the problem of scratched records, warped records, and records with various substances accidentally stuck to the best tracks.

I remember The Beach Boys singing *Good Vibrations.*

I remember a friend of mine standing on a bridge over a busy road and saying he could feel black vibes.

I remember someone saying that inside every silver lining there was a big black cloud.

I remember a bumper sticker that read: I'M NOT PARANOID. WHO SAID I WAS?

I remember the sex-saturated, wildly anxious atmosphere of Crumb cartoons.

I remember "the hairy left".

I remember the group bedroom in a commune with everyone's bed lined up side by side.

I remember when some girls didn't shave their legs or their armpits, and wore tie-dye dresses that matched their curtains.

I remember the girl who cycled naked down the street in Johannesburg.

I remember a cramped little house in Braamfontein with LOVE, BE LOVING, LOVINGLY painted across the front wall.

I remember:
> Yummy yummy yummy
> I've got love in my tummy.

I remember when some of my friends went on a grape diet and the skins made them sick.

I remember the girl who scandalised her mother by coming back from the Magaliesberg with tanned breasts.

I remember a girl swimming naked in a pool at Tonkwani gorge. She looked like a beautiful animal in a transparent egg.

I remember the group pressure to swim naked in Tonkwani gorge.

I remember when the English language was suddenly a minefield because you never knew when you were going to say something that made it seem as if you were: a) treating a girl as if she was an object, b) treating an object as if it was a girl, c) using a word like "mankind" and excluding half the human race, d) under the illusion that you were doing none of the above.

I remember a riddle which you couldn't solve if you thought (without thinking) that the surgeon must be a man when in fact she was a woman.

I remember Male Chauvinist Pigs.

I remember the girl who firmly told a mystified supermarket cashier that plastic bags were bad.

I remember thick square-bottomed paper bags that you could really pop.

I remember everyone lining up to do a chicken parade at high-school.

I remember children playing "chicken" and being run over.

I remember trying to understand why the red substance you could melt against the flap of an envelope was called "ceiling wax".

I remember liquid amber glue in small bottles with an angled red rubber top; squishing the top against a page, and either nothing or too much leaking out.

I remember conical glass bottles of sperm-coloured office glue, with a brush attached to the lid.

I remember what happened to the delegation of Wits students who went off to Pretoria to try and get a petition signed by Prime Minister B.J.Vorster: they were tarred and feathered by a bunch of Tukkies.

I remember the girl who was felled by an egg thrown from a passing car while standing in a Wits student protest on Jan Smuts Avenue.

I remember a small second-hand leftwing bookshop somewhere not far from the centre of Johannesburg, with lots of books and hardly any customers.

I remember Fanny Klenerman, warrior queen of Vanguard Bookshop.

I remember Herbert Marcuse's *One Dimensional Man*.

I remember when everyone had the silver Penguin edition of Salinger's *The Catcher in the Rye*.

I remember when people read e. e. cummings and stopped using capital letters and punctuation

I remember Don Marquis' *archie and mehitabel.*

I remember big old black Remington typewriters, sleek portable Olivetti's, carbon paper, carbon copies and corrector fluid.

I remember silver daisy wheels on electric typewriters and golf balls on I.B.M. typewriters.

I remember the slow bright floating procession of balloons at the end of *The Red Balloon.*

I remember when people stuck plastic oranges on the tips of car aerials.

I remember the false gaudy fleece spread across car dashboards.

I remember toy sausage dogs nodding their heads at the back of cars.

I remember secretly, guiltily taking my little brother with me by bus to a smoky snooker saloon in Rosebank on a Jewish holiday.

I remember an orang-outang at the zoo smoking cigarettes that were tossed to him.

I remember when my mother discovered that the white woman employed to look after my brother and sister was an alcoholic, and that the Wilson's XXX Mints she had been chewing non-stop were meant to hide the smell.

I remember when we wondered if the pieces of a body discovered floating in plastic bags in the Zoo Lake weren't her.

I remember that when our house was raided, my mother hid some documents under the mattress where my little brother was sleeping, and warned the police that if they went into his room and woke him up there would be hell to pay. (They didn't.)

I remember the delicious apple pies made by the white woman who was working for us at the time of my father's arrest.

I remember how happy she was to give the police what little information she had.

I remember DANGER/GEVAAR/INGOZI signs with a skull and cross-bones.

I remember bucket bombs used to scatter illegal leaflets.

I remember books exploding through the air at the end of *Zabriski Point*.

I remember banknotes drifting out of a hollow pumpkin in *The Magic Garden*, the first film I ever saw with black South African actors.

I remember that I never once saw a film crew in the streets of Johannesburg.

I remember frost-covered sheets of right-wing propaganda discovered in the early hours on the grass of Wits campus.

I remember the REMEMBER SHARPEVILLE banner, strung up between poles facing the Wits Central Block, and torn down by a raging mob of students.

I remember various slogans painted on paths and walls of the campus in the dead of night, such as A SQUARE PIG IN A ROUND HOLE, and HALITOSIS IS THE LAST LINE OF DEFENCE.

I remember the suspicion of spying that fell on the heads of any number of students, and that at least one of those who later turned out to really be a spy, hadn't been suspected at all.

I remember her putting her cool hands over my eyes from behind on the Wits library lawn and saying "Guess who?" (I couldn't.)

I remember Jane Fonda and Donald Sutherland in *Klute*.

I remember *The Spy Who Came In From the Cold*: the yellow cover of the Gollancz hardback and the film with Richard Burton and Claire Bloom.

I remember grey photographs of the Berlin wall, with barbed wire and look-out posts, and articles about people being shot while trying cross over.

I remember:
> Spring is sprung,
> The grass is grizz,
> I wonder where the boidies is?
> The boid is on the wing.
> But that's absoid!
> The wing is on the boid.

I remember the sperm smell of the chestnut tree on the library lawn at the beginning of summer, just when we were supposed to be studying for exams.

I remember recognising from afar the cocky voice of the young man who was marching a platoon of drum majorettes under the trees on campus. He had been my corporal in the army.

I remember the Wits Rag, the Rag Queen, and floats nosing majestically through the middle of town.

I remember a group of men dressed up as St. Stithian's hockey players with very visible garters to their very laddered black stockings, trying to play hockey with the coins that were thrown to them.

I remember the *Rag Mag*, and STUNG stickers for your car windscreen if you bought one.

I remember the 90-day detention law, the 180-day detention law, and CHARGE OR RELEASE stickers.

I remember that, after we'd been to a café with my sister and some friends on her birthday, the owner sent my mother's cheque back to her with a note which read something like: "On the understanding that this birthday was for the daughter of the man who taught me physics at Wits."

I remember when no one had a computer except the Wits computer department, and people who worked there made print-outs of Marilyn Monroe's face on pale blue or green and white-lined paper.

I remember when shocking pink and phosphorescent green were in.

I remember the poster of Frank Zappa sitting on the toilet.

I remember a student bedroom with cult posters, potent quotes pinned on the inside of built-in wardrobes, the walls shaking with acid rock. And somewhere else in the spotless, sterile interior, the parents.

I remember Dibs.

I remember Mary Barnes, R.D. Laing's *The Politics of Experience* and *Knots*. Primal scream therapy. And a woman threatening me with gut therapy.

I remember Carl Rodgers, day-long T-group sessions in hot prefabs, and paper-board diagrams of group behaviour drawn with Cokey pens.

I remember the intrigue and boredom of N.U.S.A.S. conferences.

I remember Steve Biko's smile.

I remember when Jonny Wacks played a song with a chorus that went "… so love me, love me, love me, I'm a liberal" to a tune by Phil Ochs during a student meeting at the Great Hall.

I remember that the first time I saw Johnny Clegg he came on stage with his guitar at The Blue Fox Hotel in Rosebank as part of the supporting programme for Phil Ochs, along with Paul Clingman and Edie Nederlander, and announced that he was going to sing a song in Zulu about rat poison.

I remember hecklers at meetings in the Wits Great Hall, especially the moment when S.R.C. member Ray Wacks was interrupted by one more "Get your hair cut!" from the engineers and he flung back "Get your throat cut!"

I remember little trolls with soft blue or pink hair.

I remember battles on an English beach between the Mods and the Rockers.

I remember that Mick Jagger was a student at the London School of Economics.

I remember Dennis Brutus, Peter Hain and press photos of overseas sports pitches invaded by anti-apartheid protesters.

I remember how you weren't supposed to "mix sport and politics".

I remember the scandal when Basil "Dolly" D'Oliviera was picked for the English cricket tour of South Africa.

I remember Yvonne Goolagong.

I remember when I thought that G-strings were made of wire, even when women wore them.

I remember "pocket billiards" and "piepie jawlers".

I remember peeling away the hard skin of golf-balls, boiling them and then splitting the rubber threads underneath to get to the little rubber bag of thick, milky liquid at the center.

I remember rolling balls out of warm tar at the side of the road.

I remember the taste of tepid water in a plastic water-bottle during a long hike.

I remember:
>   I left, I left, I left my wife and seventy kids,
>   The silly old bitch she'll never get rich.

I remember going on the *The Rand Daily Mail* 25-kilometre Walk between Johannesburg and Pretoria with my father in jail at the far end, and never getting any closer to him.

I remember Nancy Sinatra singing "These boots are made for walking."

I remember Otis Redding singing *Sitting in the Dock of the Bay*.

I remember how to tell the difference between stalactites and stalagmites: the tights come down and the mites crawl up.

I remember Canadian lumber jackets with small red and black checks.

I remember the Canadian Army fitness book.

I remember "I wish you well to wear it".

I remember "Many happy returns of the day".

I remember Scalectrix racing circuits.

I remember the way you could get a Subbuteo player to curve back and tap the ball forward.

I remember "Yirra!" and "Yirra Piet!" with a long, satisfying roll of the "r" and a shake of the head.

I remember the game of "sardines", when you hid and whoever found you hid with you.

I remember sardine tins with keys.

I remember the irresistible attraction of lucky dips.

I remember compressed cubes of Turkish dates wrapped in cellophane that sometimes didn't come unstuck.

I remember the acid-sweet taste of little Pez sweets, and their plastic flip-open distributors.

I remember Chappies bubble-gum with Did You Know? questions on the wrapper, and Wick's which was thick and pink and covered in fine white powder.

I remember jumping beans.

I remember the warm sweet relief of peeing into your pyjamas when you were hardly awake, and the dawning horror of what you had done to your bed.

I remember my maroon rubberised under-blanket.

I remember what might have been my first song, "Mmm Mmm Mmm Hmm" (with the first three notes the same and the last note rising), while I sucked a little green square of mohair, all that was left of my "baby-blanket".

I remember "Upsidaisy!".

I remember the pleasure of pulling feathers out of an eiderdown.

I remember a girl pulling my hair so hard I couldn't even scream.

I remember itchy powder from plane tree pom-poms, peeled willow tree whips and paper water bombs.

I remember false teeth made of inside-out naartjie peel.

I remember Richmal Crompton's "William" books.

I remember books set in an English school in which a younger boy silently, almost painfully admires an older one, for chapters on end, and is finally noticed.

I remember *The Great Escape*, *The Dam Busters* and the round bomb that could bounce across water and explode against the base of a dam-wall.

I remember that Douglas Bader lost a leg in the war.

I remember Roger Bannister and the four-minute mile.

I remember my brother running into Johannesburg at the end of a relay race that started in Durban.

I remember him telling me that when you ran you could imagine that there was a bowl of water between your hips, and that you should try not to spill a drop.

I remember that Sea Cottage (the hot favourite) was shot before the Durban July.

I remember that "athlete's foot" sounded like quite a nice thing to have.

I remember those full-length newspaper photos of two boxers just before a match, with all their attributes listed side by side.

I remember Floyd Patterson and his lantern jaw.

I remember Cassius Clay's motto: "Float like a butterfly, sting like a bee".

I remember Vic Toweel.

I remember the "Fosberry flop", and Porfirio Bento who used it to break the high-jump record at our high-school.

I remember Karen Muir's wet triumphant face. I think she had freckles.

I remember how adolescent girls were attracted to life-guards.

I remember that boys could "sow wild oats", but if a girl allowed herself to sleep with a boy, he would "lose his respect for her".

I remember the whole question of whether you could love two girls at a time, which hid the other question of having to remain faithful to the girl you were with.

I remember Crosby, Stills, Nash and Young:
    Why can't we
    Get on as three?

I remember a girl who had two lovers and no telephone. A car parked outside her house would tell one of them that the other one was already in there.

I remember the main fear: that a girl might fall pregnant.

I remember spermicide jelly.

I remember the challenge of asking a suddenly stony-faced woman at the chemist's for condoms.

I remember Dr. Kildare and Richard Chamberlain, and the way there were romantic comic strips at the bottom of a full page of smalls ads.

I remember when cinema ads were sometimes just a motionless slide on the screen telling you about a local caterer, men's outfitters or ladies hairdresser.

I remember engagement rings and fiancées, and Stern's diamonds.

I remember that a beautiful spy in one of the James Bond books had fine muscular buttocks.

I remember khaki canvas school bags covered in graffiti, including an "OO7" with a gun-barrel running through the OOs.

I remember the joke about the newly married couple undressing in the bridal chamber. She says: "Look, darling: blue blouse"; "Look, darling: blue bra" ... and then he says "Look, darling, blew off in the war."

I remember Dr. Chris Barnard, his very white smile and glittering new wife. Louis Washkansky's new heart. And Philip Blaiberg's.

I remember questions in the papers about whether a white patient could receive a heart from a black donor, and something about baboon hearts.

I remember " black spots ".

I remember Beyers Naudé and a group of helpers in the northern suburbs of Johannesburg loading up a truck of provisions for the people who had been dumped at Limehill.

I remember Kupagani.

I remember Cosmas Desmond and his book about Limehill and Dimbaza.

I remember the names of people who were shot down at Sharpeville appearing in the "Obituaries" column of the newspaper ten years later.

I remember the "Cripple School" across the road from our house.

I remember Thalidomide babies.

I remember "sick notes", and forged "sick notes".

I remember "crib notes".

I remember that a couple of weeks before the matric exam I suddenly got it into my head to decorate my room with the most exotic pictures of far-off places I could find.

I remember "Top of the Pops" on the transistor radio announced by a slick voice towards the end of the afternoon, and nothing ahead but homework.

I remember Engelbert Humperdink.

I remember Eric Burdon and The Animals' version of *House of the Rising Sun.*

I remember the rumour that Patty Hearst was in love with a member of the Symbionese Liberation Army group that had kidnapped her.

I remember that kidnappers cut off the ear of Paul Getty's son and sent it to him.

I remember people wearing Bonnie and Clyde caps.

I remember that Yoko Ono did an exhibition of photos of people's bottoms.

I remember reading somewhere that on the stage set of *Cleopatra* Richard Burton called out in a stage whisper to Liz Taylor: "You're too fat."

I remember Margot Fonteyn, her diplomat husband in a wheelchair, and Rudolf Nureyev.

I remember *Lara's Theme* in *Dr. Zhivago,* and the moment when he gets out of an animal-skin bed in the early morning to sit at a table, look out at the snow and write poems while Julie Christie goes on sleeping.

I remember when she taps on the bus window but outside on the pavement he doesn't see her and has a heart attack.

I remember:
> Those were the days my friend,
> We thought they'd never end.

I remember the nagging question of what exactly we thought we were going to do when we left university.

I remember two students spending a full day in a trance out on a Wits rugby field with sunlight in their blonde hair and love in their marijuana-pink eyes.

I remember *Blow Up*, the man and the woman running across the park, and the photograph in which there was possibly a dead man hidden in the bushes.

I remember someone saying that our hormones were *much* more important than exams.

I remember that when a Wits administrator asked a friend of mine why his feet were bare he said it was because he couldn't take them off.

I remember the Wits administrator who accompanied members of the Special Branch to a lecture hall so they could arrest John Schlapobersky. And later Ian Margo's play *The Arrest of Pascal Kasnovsky*.

I remember the Brian Brooke Theatre, actors wearing too much make-up and speaking as if they had a cramp in their mouths.

I remember that if you wanted a book about an African tribe, in most bookshops you had to go to the Flora and Fauna section.

I remember Bushmen in a glass case in the Africana museum.

I remember Athol Fugard and Molly Seftel in *Hello and Goodbye*, with real white South African accents on stage.

I remember Fugard and Yvonne Bryceland in *Boesman and Lena* at the Arena, without make-up, and Yvonne Bryceland's fresh raw chuckle.

I remember Dumile's lean couples sculpted out of a single branch.

I remember the title of the book *Where White is the Colour, Where Black is the Number* by Wopko Jensma.

I remember Tessa Marwick's production of *Gilgamesh*, with all the skin and electricity.

I remember sit-ins, and drop-outs.

I remember Night School.

I remember meetings of The Johannesburg Film Society, the desolation of Hillbrow streets in the evening, and people collecting on the pavement before the film.

I remember Bunuel's *The Exterminating Angel*.

I remember when people rented plots of land in Hillbrow, and turned them into parking lots on Saturday night.

I remember when the round-the-clock Fontana Bakery opened in Hillbrow, and the discovery of shopping at night.

I remember parking meters with a green arrow moving across a dial, and a red "Expired" sign.

I remember "the brain drain".

I remember that when my father came out of prison he grew his side-burns down to the earlobes to catch up with the times.

I remember the beautiful young couple I met only once who went off sailing and were never seen again.

I remember the Union Castle Lines.

I remember Thor Heyerdal's Kon-Tiki expedition.

I remember people who had exit permits but couldn't legally reach an airport because they were confined to a magisterial district.

I remember the red plastic bag into which my mother decided to put all her important documents, in case we had to leave in a hurry.

I remember red lanterns stolen from road works in students' rooms where there wasn't much else apart from a desk, a lamp, a mattress and a bean-bag.

I remember my little sister sitting at the back of the car and saying "Look, the robot's red. We'll have to wait until spring before it turns green."

I remember braziers at night in Hillbrow. Beer brawls. And cops disguised as hippies going in and out of nightclubs.

I remember Purple Hearts.

I remember the night watchmen on campus, with khaki greatcoats and balaclavas, and knobkieries.

I remember that a night watchman caught a girl who had been out slogan painting on campus by throwing his knobkierie at her legs.

I remember the night watchman filling the doorway before the evening at the Wits Film Society began, and saying in a deep theatrical voice: "Before you go, remember: let out the cat. Cover the canary. Switch off the light."

I remember Jan Smuts Airport on the afternoon we left. A heavy yellow lozenge of light reflected from a window onto the concourse floor. A policeman in a khaki uniform standing against a wall. The remoteness of the crowds.

I remember the girl who said "The night will swallow me and spit out the pips."

Postscript

Imagine you are in an aeroplane at daybreak. You have just woken up to an announcement by the pilot that the long flight will be over in a few minutes. A city tilts towards you as the plane approaches. You catch a glimpse of street-lamps, cars silently torching the soft grey air, a few yellow windows in the massed darkness of buildings. You are filled with the presence of this place as it stirs from the intimacy of the night.

Now imagine that what you are looking at is not a city of the present but a city of the past, your past; a place you have not lived in for decades, and which you are returning to as if it continued to be all it had ever been before you left. The lights you see are your own glittering, floating memories, stretching across the years, some of them highly personal, others shared with neighbours, schoolmates, people you might never even have met but who once lived in the same place at the same time as you did.

These memories rise into focus across the foggy gap of absence. Together, they trace the map of a city that shines more and more compellingly in your mind, closer than a jewelled runway below an aeroplane as it lands.

This is the experience I had not so long ago, triggered by a book I read. The memories that kept coming back to me with increasing insistence were mainly of South Africa when I was growing up there in the 1950s, 60s and early 70s. The book, however, made no mention of this country at all.

It was called *Je me souviens* (I Remember) by Georges Perec, and contained 480 brief, numbered entries, most of them connected with a fifteen year period after 1946. This was the year when Perec came back to Paris at the age of ten, having spent three years in the "free zone" to avoid capture by the Nazis.

Je me souviens is in many ways a celebration of the return to normality in this city; it is filled with references to jazz and cinema, fashion, sport, radio programmes and bistros. But it is also a book which, on closer inspection, pays a price for this celebration: though concerned with memory, it barely touches on the Second World War, during which Perec lost most of his immediate family. His father died in uniform one week before the Franco-German armistice; his mother did not survive Auschwitz.

In other words, *Je me souviens* is also, in ways that intimately concern its author, a book of forgetting. The tension between remembering and forgetting, between unmentionable personal loss and relief at the buoyancy of the post-war years, is perhaps part of what drew me to this book. I suspect, though, that beyond the actual content, it was the structure of *Je me souviens* that triggered my own memories.

Here was a way of setting down in brief, pointillist fashion the details of a gone world, creating a pattern that seemed to reflect the syntax of memory itself. The sequence of Perec's notation is unpredictable, elliptical, pursuing a divergent series of paths, zigzagging between different subjects, time-periods, widening in scope by way of invisible association.

Remembering is an activity that takes place from several angles at once, the mind constantly shifting perspective. It also involves a complementary tendency to focus on individual details, sometimes of the most banal and forgettable variety, but which turn out to be keyholes through which entire landscapes can be glimpsed. *Je me souviens* is made up of both these aspects simultaneously.

Perec borrowed this method from the American Joe Brainard, who in the early 1970s created a frank, created a capricious, frank and uproariously funny autobiographical mosaic of his brief recollections, constantly returning to his central theme: colourfully explicit male sexual encounters.

If Brainard was flamboyantly transgressing the taboo surrounding homosexuality, Perec buried his own identity (which he writes of powerfully elsewhere) behind a far less personal set of elements, a collective inventory of mental souvenirs. His was an utterly discrete, tempered exercise, as befitted not only his purpose but also the highly codified relations and protective *pudeur* of the culture he was writing out of.

Whatever their differences, however, both men produced essentially poetic works. The rhetorical device of repeating over and over again the phrase "Je me souviens" or "I remember" eventually turns the text into a sort of incantation. The reader, like the writer, might not only discover long-hidden memories, but also come to recognise and even succumb to the hypnotic strength of the act of remembering itself.

By the time one has gone through a few hundred sentences beginning "I remember", the "I" might have dissolved in the remembering. Memory then becomes a potentially more selfless place, a shared city that can be seen with greater clarity than when one actually lived there. But of course one never actually lived there. The city of memory is always somewhere else.

Denis Hirson was born in Cambridge, England, of South African parents in 1951. He lived in South Africa from 1952 until 1973, the year in which his father, who had been a political prisoner, was released from jail. He studied Social Anthropology at the University of the Witwatersrand, and has since worked as an actor and English teacher in France.

In addition to his mosaic of memory, *The House Next Door to Africa*, he has edited an anthology of South African poetry, *The Lava of this Land*; co-edited *The Heinemann Book of South African Short Stories*, with Martin Trump; and translated into English a selection of Breyten Breytenbach's poetry, *In Africa Even the Flies are Happy*.

He lives just outside Paris with his wife Adine Sagalyn, and children Anna and Jeremy.